THE ARABIC LANGUAGE TODAY

Modern Languages

Editor

R. AUTY

M.A., DR.PHIL.

Professor of Comparative Slavonic Philology
in the University of Oxford

THE ARABIC LANGUAGE TODAY

A. F. L. Beeston
Laudian Professor of Arabic
University of Oxford

HUTCHINSON UNIVERSITY LIBRARY
LONDON

HUTCHINSON & CO (*Publishers*) LTD
178–202 Great Portland Street, London W.1

London Melbourne Sydney
Auckland Johannesburg Cape Town
and agencies throughout the world

First published 1970

This book has been set in Times New Roman type face. It has been printed in Great Britain by William Clowes and Sons Ltd, London and Beccles, on Smooth Wove paper and bound by Wm. Brendon of Tiptree, Essex

ISBN 0 09 103100 1 (cased)
0 09 103101 X (paper)

CONTENTS

PREFACE

When I was invited to contribute to this series, I had just published a concise manual of Arabic.[1] In the course of working on that, I had done a good deal of thinking on underlying principles, but much of this had to be excluded from the published book both for the sake of conciseness and because the book was designed for strictly practical ends. But I had debated the possibility of embodying my thoughts in another work aimed at those interested in examining the language from a more theoretical standpoint; and the invitation offered me a welcome opportunity of doing this.

As a result, however, I find myself here addressing two distinct types of reader: first, general and comparative linguists wishing to gain an idea of how Arabic works; and secondly, those with some practical knowledge of the language who wish to know more about its theoretical bases. For the former, I have had to include material which will be all too familiar to the practical Arabist; for the latter, some general linguistic statements which will appear very trite to the professional linguist, as well as some detail with which he will no doubt feel he could have dispensed. To both therefore I have to apologize and ask for their forbearance. Moreover, anyone who approaches this book after reading *Written Arabic* will find that some of my formulations here differ slightly from those which, for the sake of simplicity, I adopted there; but in all cases of conflict, the present work represents my second thoughts.

Once again it must be said (as I said in the Introduction to *Written Arabic*, p. 4) that grammatical terminology presents an almost insuperable problem. The terminology of this book is naturally more

[1] *Written Arabic, an approach to the basic structures.*

elaborate than that needed for *Written Arabic*, but I have striven to explain it as I go along. It may however be useful to those who are not professional linguists to explain that a phoneme is an acoustic item which serves to distinguish one word from another, while a morpheme is an acoustic item which is a minimal meaningful unit: hence the *r* of English *rooks* is a distinct phoneme from the *l* of *looks*, but is not phonemically distinct in English from the guttural 'Parisian' *r* which can be used in place of the normal *r*; the *s* is a morpheme because it conveys an isolable unit of meaning (here plurality), contrasting with *rook*.

In order to illustrate the structural features of Arabic, I have had recourse to phrases modelled on the Arabic structural pattern and placed within angular brackets to distinguish them from the correct English translation, which is placed in quotes.

Obviously, a work of this nature is selective and makes no attempt to cover exhaustively all the phenomena of the language.

I

INTRODUCTION AND HISTORICAL BACKGROUND

Arabic is the official language of Morocco, Algeria, Tunis, Libya, the United Arab Republic, Sudan, Lebanon, Syria, Jordan, Iraq and the states of the Arabian peninsula. Within these political frontiers the only substantial bodies of non-Arabic speakers are the Berbers of North Africa (most of whom are now bilingual in Arabic and Berber), speakers of Kurdish (an Iranian dialect) in the north of Iraq and Syria, and the tribal populations of the southern Sudan. Outside of them, Arabic is used in Israel, in the south-western corner of Iran, in some enclaves in the Central Asian republics of the Soviet Union, and in some areas fringing the south of the Sahara. As the language of the Qur'ān, Arabic is to some extent familiar throughout the Muslim world, rather as Latin is in the lands of the Roman Church; less so in Turkey, where official policy since 1923 has aimed at replacing it by Turkish.

The term 'Arabic' is applied to a number of speech-forms which, in spite of many and sometimes substantial mutual differences, possess sufficient homogeneity to warrant their being reckoned as dialectal varieties of a single language. There is one fundamental division of these varieties. On the one hand, we find localized varieties employed in the speech of everyday life, which have been frequently termed 'the Arabic dialects', but would be better designated 'vernaculars'. These form a continuous spectrum of variation, of which the extremities, Moroccan and Iraqi, differ to the point of mutual unintelligibility, but within which one variety shades off almost imperceptibly into the adjoining one. The vernaculars are almost entirely spoken forms of language; a few attempts have been made at rendering them in writing, but Arabic script is ill-adapted for this purpose, and such attempts have no greater linguistic value than an English novelist's attempts at recording, say, Lancashire dialect. Linguistic descriptions of the vernaculars are invariably in phonetic transcription.

Sharply contrasted with the vernaculars is a variety of language used throughout the whole Arabic-speaking world, and which forms the normal vehicle for all written communication. Many labels have been used for this, none entirely satisfactory. It has been called 'classical', though some of its manifestations are difficult to fit into any normal acceptance of that term; it has been called 'literary', in spite of the fact that many of its manifestations—newspaper advertisements, for instance—have nothing to do with literature; it has been called 'written', and yet it is frequently used as a medium for spoken communication, as in formal speeches and in radio broadcasts aimed at the whole Arab world; it can be called 'standard', though even this leads to difficulty when one looks at the language historically and not solely in the light of current circumstances. In default of a more satisfactory term, 'Standard Arabic' (SA) is in this work used for this variety of the language.

Up to the present, it is the vernaculars which have attracted most attention from linguists, and there is a very large bibliography devoted to them.[1] Relatively little work has been done, in terms of structural analysis, on SA,[2] and it is the latter which is the subject of the present book.

Some brief mention should be made of Maltese, which is anomalous. In spite of heavy lexical infiltration from Italian, Maltese is unquestionably an Arabic vernacular. But for nearly a thousand years, Malta has been politically and culturally sundered from North Africa, and from contact with any other variety of the language. At the end of the eighteenth century, when it was first reduced to writing, Latin script was chosen, and it has now evolved (the only Arabic vernacular to do so) into a literary language with its own traditions. In consequence, SA is unused and unintelligible in Malta.

Historical background

Arabic belongs to the language-family commonly called Semitic. Other principal members of the family are Ugaritic and Accadian (both now long dead), Aramaic (surviving only in vestigial form),

[1] The most recent, and probably most generally useful, works on the vernaculars are the series of analytical descriptions published by the Georgetown University Institute of Languages and Linguistics, of which volumes on Moroccan, Syrian and Iraqi have appeared. For Egyptian, the best book available at present is T. F. Mitchell's *Introduction to Egyptian Colloquial Arabic* (Oxford University Press, 1956), though this is pedagogical and not systematic as the Georgetown series is.

[2] But one cannot omit reference to V. Monteil's very valuable *L'arabe moderne*.

Hebrew, and the Semitic languages of Ethiopia (Tigre, Tigrina, Amharic, and the church language Geez). In the north and centre of the Arabian peninsula, a range of inscriptions datable from roughly the fifth century B.C. to the fifth century A.D. exhibit a group of dialects which are probably the ancestors of Arabic as we know it, although they cannot be termed Arabic any more than Anglo-Saxon could be termed English. The dialects of pre-Islamic South Arabia are a separate language within the Semitic family, and not in any sense ancestors of Arabic.

The earliest manifestation of a linguistic form which can be identified as Arabic is on a tombstone at Nemara in the Syrian desert, dated A.D. 328, and one or two similar inscriptions from the fifth–sixth century. Round about A.D. 600 there were current in Arabia a number of dialects, roughly classifiable into an eastern and a western group; our information about these dialects is confined to a number of scattered and unorganized remarks by later Muslim philologists. The course of the sixth century, however, had seen the production of a corpus of poetry, preserved initially by oral transmission, and only written down for the first time in the eighth–ninth century; the linguistic status of this poetic corpus is very debatable, but a frequently accepted hypothesis is that it represents a sort of *koine* or common language used for poetry (and probably for 'elevated' diction in general) throughout the peninsula, and not completely identifiable with any one dialect as used for the purposes of everyday life, though on the whole its main features appear to be eastern rather than western.

In the early years of the seventh century the Qur'ān, Islam's sacred book, was revealed to the Prophet Muhammad. The revelations were memorized by his followers and also written down by amanuenses; the Qur'ān is therefore the earliest surviving document of written Arabic, apart from the few inscriptions which have been mentioned above. Its language is unmistakably that of the poetic corpus of the sixth century. Nevertheless, it was first written down in a form reflecting the pronunciation of the western dialect of Mecca, and it was not until nearly a century later that the scholars of Lower Iraq succeeded in imposing on the pronunciation used for its recitation certain features characteristic of the eastern dialects. This they did, not by altering the primitive written text but by adding reading marks to it, a process which has resulted in some of the oddities of Arabic script as used at the present day.

From the early years of Islam we possess a number of written documents, both of a formal kind (inscriptions, tombstones, coins, etc.) and of an informal kind such as letters and contracts. The former evidently aim at being written in Quranic language, the latter often show divergences from it attributable to dialectal influences. Poetic literature continued to be produced and transmitted orally in the same manner as it had been before the advent of Islam. And the vast body of traditions relative to the life and sayings of the Prophet constitute the beginning of a prose literature.

Quite apart, however, from the fact that the Tradition literature includes some material forged at a later date, a linguist must use it with a good deal of caution. For it, like the poetry, was at first transmitted orally and only written down at a later stage; and although later scholars who handled it then laid stress on verbal accuracy, it is manifest that the contemporaries of the Prophet had no such idea, but concerned themselves only with the content of the record, not with its precise linguistic form of expression. We can see this in the fact that traditions are sometimes recorded for us by the later scholars in several forms which, while conveying the same ultimate sense, differ in verbal expression.

Soon after A.D. 700 a great change came over the situation. The Muslim conquests had dispersed Arab settlers over a vast stretch of territory from Spain to Eastern Persia, and this led to a blurring of the old dialectal distinctions; though, therefore, there are isolated features in the modern vernaculars which can be envisaged as stemming from the dialects of the Arabian peninsula in the Prophet's day, no one modern vernacular can be safely asserted to have developed out of any one ancient dialect of the peninsula.

More important, the Muslim conquests resulted in the adoption of the use of Arabic by vast numbers of non-Arabs, among whom were to be found the intellectual élite of the Muslim world; and this led to a very rapid and significant evolution in the common language itself.

The eighth-century scholars, specially in Lower Iraq, were keenly aware of this development, but greatly apprehensive of it; for they judged that an unhampered evolution of this kind would lead in the end to a loss of ability to understand the Qur'ān and the Prophetic Tradition, just as in fact the evolution of the Romance languages has led to Latin becoming a dead language for most Europeans. Hence were born in that century the sciences of Arabic grammar and lexicography, of which a principal aim was to establish a standard of 'correct' Arabic. The grammar taught in the schools of the Arab world today is virtually identical with the grammatical system devised by the eighth-century scholars; and throughout the period from then to now this grammar has been the ideal aimed at by the educated classes for literary expression.

Contemporary with the birth of the grammatical sciences was the efflorescence of a 'golden age' of Arabic literature, which stretched on into the eleventh century. The great bulk of all that has been considered best in Arabic literature is the product of this age, in which a series of brilliant writers forged, out of the relatively unsophisticated language of earlier times, an instrument of marvellous subtlety for expressing the finest shades of meaning.

The twelfth–eighteenth centuries were, relatively speaking, an age of decadence, marked only by the occasional appearance of a truly great writer. But in the middle of the nineteenth century a literary renaissance (the so-called *nahḍa* movement) took place, beginning in Lebanon, spreading to Egypt, and thence to other parts of the Arab world. The founders of this movement looked for their inspiration and models to the great writers of the golden age; and among their main activities were the publication of reliable texts of golden age writers, the 'rediscovery' of writers whose works had fallen into oblivion during the decadence, and the compilation of dictionaries of 'correct' lexical usage. As a result of this activity, SA is in its main features modelled on the language of the golden age writers.

Yet there is an inherent contradiction here. At the moment when the grammarians set to work, the common language had already changed from that of the Tradition literature, and had probably never been wholly identical with the 'elevated' style of poetry and the Qur'ān on which the grammarians mainly based themselves. A purely synchronic analysis of golden age prose writing would probably have resulted in a system differing in some details from that worked out by the grammarians.

But simultaneously with the *nahḍa* movement, a challenge was facing the Arab world as great as it had encountered in the eighth century. Just as, then, the ancient bedouin Arabian culture was being profoundly modified by urbanization and the consequent demand for expression of new modes of thought, so in the nineteenth century the centuries-old Muslim–Arab culture had to face the challenge of European culture and new modes of thought demanding new modes of expression. Yet while, obviously, these demands have had a tremendous influence on the lexicon, the structural and morphological features of the language have remained remarkably stable—partly because of the emotional appeal of the link with the Prophetic age, and partly because of the excellence of the golden age language as a tool of expression. There is even detectable in some modern writers an archaizing tendency towards re-introducing some features of ancient Arabic which had virtually disappeared from the language of the golden age (see e.g. pp. 100[1], 105).

2

PHONOLOGY

The phonemic repertory

The phonemic repertory of SA consists of the following items:

(1) Three vowel-qualities, open, palatal and lip-rounded.
(2) Twenty-four consonants.
(3) A phonetic feature known to the Arabs as *'iṭbāq*, which occurs simultaneously with four of the consonants, thus raising the effective consonantism to twenty-eight items (the reason for not registering simply twenty-eight consonants will appear below).
(4) The quality of length, applicable to all vowels and all consonants. This is a temporal extension of the duration of the sound; but while this is a full statement in the case of vowels and continuant consonants, such as *f*, in the case of 'stops' the extension affects only the period of 'closure' (see below) preceding the faint explosion of breath which occurs when the closure is released. When morphological structure brings two identical consonants into immediate contact, this gives rise to lengthening of the consonant, so that $t + t$ produces a long *t* and not an articulation with two separate explosions. Nevertheless, from the point of view of Arabic morphological structure, a lengthened consonant has exactly the same value as two consonants.

The Arabic script is constituted on strictly phonemic principles, and provides notation only for sounds with phonemic value. The phonetic realization of the phonemes is a more complicated matter than would appear from the script.

The three vowel qualities cover a wide range of phonetic realizations. To the English ear, the most noticeable case is that of the open quality vowel, which ranges from a pure open */a/* with mouth opened to maximum extent, as in English 'car', to a distinctly flattened vowel /*æ*/ somewhat resembling the vowel of standard southern English 'cat'. The palatal quality ranges from a narrowly closed vowel similar to that of French 'pique', to relaxed varieties resembling the vowel of English 'pit' and Russian ы. The lip-rounded quality ranges from a narrowly closed /*u*/ particularly in its lengthened form, to a more relaxed sound when not lengthened; a fact which leads Europeans often to hear the short variety of the lip-rounded vowel as the /*o*/ vowel of French 'Monet'. These varieties of articulation are positionally determined and in no case do they serve, by themselves, the phonemic function of distinguishing one word from another.

All consonants involve some degree of closure or obstruction to the free passage of the breath through the mouth; the closure is complete in the case of 'stops' and approximative in 'continuants'. A convenient primary classification is based on the speech-organs with which the obstruction is effected; other classificatory features are 'voicing' (concurrent vibration of the vocal chords), 'unvoicing' (suspension of that vibration), nasalization, and others which will be explained as they occur. The primary classification yields:

(i) bilabials, with obstruction between the two lips:

b, voiced stop;
m, voiced nasalized stop;
w, semivowel (on which see below).

(ii) labio-dental, between lower lip and upper teeth:

f, unvoiced continuant.

(iii) linguals, of which the tongue-tip is the lower member, and subdivided according to the upper member into

(a) dentals, back of the upper teeth:

t, unvoiced stop;
d, voiced stop;
t̠, unvoiced continuant as English 'th' in 'thing';
d̠, voiced continuant as English 'th' in 'that';
l, voiced lateralized semi-continuant, the centre of the tongue being in full closure, but the breath allowed to escape at the sides.

(b) dental-alveolars, at the base of the upper teeth:

s, unvoiced continuant hiss;
z, voiced continuant buzz.

(c) alveolars, on the gum-ridge behind the teeth:

š̆, unvoiced continuant with retroflexion of tongue-tip, similar to English 'sh';
n, voiced nasalized stop;
r, voiced trill, with the tongue repeatedly tapped against the gum-ridge as in Spanish 'r'.

(d) velarized alveolars, a variety of *t s z* and *d* or *d̲*, with the tongue-tip further back and with the concurrent phenomenon of *'iṭbāq*, which is a buccal resonance caused by raising the back part of the tongue towards the soft palate:

ṭ, unvoiced stop;
ṣ, unvoiced continuant;
ẓ, voiced continuant;
ḍ, voiced stop or continuant.[1]

(iv) palatals, between the centre of the tongue and the upper palate:

j, voiced continuant with explosive onset, as in English 'j';[2]
y, semivowel.

(v) velars, between back of the tongue and back part of palate:

k, unvoiced stop;
k̲, unvoiced continuant, as German 'ch' in 'Bach';
ḡ, voiced continuant, the French 'Parisian r'.

(vi) uvular, with point of obstruction further back than with the velars:

q, unvoiced stop.

(vii) pharyngals, with obstruction of the pharyngal passage:

ḥ, unvoiced continuant;
', voiced continuant.

[1] There is some fluctuation in the realization of this phoneme. Ancient descriptions of it suggest that it may have had a lateralized quality; and indeed in an Arabic loanword in Spanish such as *alcalde* the *ld* is an attempt to represent this phoneme. In modern times, some speakers realize it as a stop, some as a continuant, that is, a velarized equivalent of *d̲*; the less educated confuse it with *ẓ*, since in many of the vernaculars there has been a complete loss of phonemic distinction between the two. See W. Magee, 'Pronunciation of prelingual mutes in classical Arabic', in *Word*.

[2] In ancient Arabic this was a voiced stop like English 'g' in 'get', and this realization survives in the Egyptian vernacular, and is often used by Egyptians even when speaking SA. Similarly Syrians often employ the realization characteristic of their own vernacular, namely French 'j' (/*ž*/).

(viii) glottals, articulated in the glottis:

h, unvoiced continuant, fairly similar to English 'h';

', unvoiced stop; this is the German 'Vokalanstoss' as heard before every initial vowel in correct 'Bühnendeutsch'; it can also be heard in some English dialects, such as Cockney and Glaswegian, as a substitute for intervocalic *t*—the Glaswegian enunciation of 'water' illustrates it very well. It is called by the Arabs *hamz*.

The semivowels *w* and *y* stand to some extent apart from the rest of the system. Phonologically, they are hardly distinguishable from the vowels *u* and *i*; it is only their syllabic context which validates their status as consonants. As a result, they are reckoned 'weak' consonants, and in some morphological patterns they reduce to zero or are reflected only in vowel changes. Provided, however, that their syllabic context is appropriate, and that they have not been reduced on the morphological plane, they are fully functioning consonants.

As remarked above, the realization of the phonemes listed hitherto exhibits more variety than the phonemic list implies. In particular, *'iṭbāq* is not in phonetic reality simply a component of the four velarized alveolar consonants; it is a 'prosody' of which the minimal length is a consonant + vowel segment, and sometimes longer. All consonants of groups (i) to (iii, c) have velarized and non-velarized varieties according to whether or not they are included in a segment of utterance to which the velarization feature applies. The variations in vowel realization mentioned above are conditioned by this factor to a large extent. The pure open /*a*/ is heard in a velarized segment of utterance, the flattened variety elsewhere; and the realization of the palatal quality vowel is also affected.

Although any one of the four velarized alveolar phonemes is always accompanied by some extension of the velarization feature (in that case *minimally* three phonemes, i.e. consonant plus preceding and following vowels), it occurs sometimes apart from the presence of one of those four: *r* *ḵ* *ḡ* and *q* are accompanied by a minimal extension consisting of consonant + vowel; and the word Allah has velarization resulting in the use of open /*a*/ and a velarized, 'dark', variety of *l*.[1]

It would be possible to regard *w* with *u*, and *y* with *i*, as each constituting a single phoneme *W*, *Y*, realizable as consonant or vowel according to the syllabic context. One could then say that, within the boundaries of any one syllable, *W* and *Y* as first phoneme in the syllable always have consonantal value, as second phoneme always

[1] See exhaustively D. H. Obrecht, *Effects of the second formant*; and more simply, W. H. T. Gairdner, *The Phonetics of Arabic*, ch. 7.

vowel value. The Arab theoreticians also treat *W* and *Y* as third phoneme in the syllable as consonants, so that *faY* and *fiY* are envisaged as *fay* and *fiy* and not as *fai* and *fī*. This approach, which tends towards eliminating the concept of a diphthong or a long vowel altogether from the morphological system, would have entailed difficulties with *ā*, had it not been for the fact that the conventions of the script have assigned to one, originally consonantal, letter of the alphabet the function of denoting length in the open quality vowel (p. 26); it is thereby possible to regard the vowel-length marking function of this letter as parallel to the function of *w* and *y* as third phoneme in the syllable, and so in all cases to treat *cv̄* formally as an instance of *cvc*.

Syllable structure

Syllabic analysis has a practical value in verse, where it is the basis of the metrical system. Otherwise, it is only useful as a device for the theoretical explanation of certain other phenomena, such as those of word-juncture, accent, etc.

No syllable in SA begins with *v*, *cc* or *c̄*; one must therefore make the syllabic divisions *ma/lik*, *mas/jid*, *jad/da*. Within any stretch of junctured utterance, the only admissible syllabic structures are *cv*, *cv̄* and *cvc*. Before a break in utterance, or pause, the structures *cv̄c* and *cvcc* are also admitted. Any situation which would result in *cv̄c* occurring otherwise than before a pause is normally avoided by realizing the syllable as *cvc*: the closely junctured phrase *fī* + *lmadā* is actualized in utterance (though not in script) as *fil/ma/dā*. There are, however, a few instances in which the contrast between *cvc* and *cv̄c* is meaningful and the maintenance of the contrast demands the admissibility of the syllabic structure *cv̄c* otherwise than before a pause: *jad/da* 'grandmother' versus *jād/da* 'road', *kā/ti/bul/wa/ṯī/qa* 'the writer of the document' versus *kā/ti/būl/wa/ṯī/qa* 'the writers of the document'.

Neutralization of length

Quite apart from the phenomenon of neutralization of the phoneme of vowel length just mentioned, there is a tendency in ordinary rapid SA diction to neutralize the length phoneme, both in consonants and vowels, in word-final position; the length of a word-final consonant or vowel is indeterminate (a feature strongly marked in the vernaculars), and only in careful and deliberate enunciation would it be possible to detect the phoneme of length in *badā* and *maḥall*.

Accent

Word accent, involving stress and tone prominence of a given syllable, is strongly marked in all varieties of Arabic; but in SA it has no phonemic value, and no two words are *solely* distinguishable by the place of the accent.

Generally speaking, the accent falls always on the ultimate syllable of the word if that syllable is *cv̄c*, *cvcc* or *cvc̄*, as in *salā́m*, *sinnáwr*, *maḥáll*.[1] Otherwise, accent is always penultimate, as in *sayyā́ra*, *qanṭára*, except in two cases:

(i) when both penultimate and antepenultimate are *cv*, the antepenultimate is accented, as in *ʿámala*.

(ii) some speakers, but not all, accent antepenultimate *cv̄* when the penultimate is *cv*, so there is fluctuation between *šā́hadū* and *šāhádū*; and a few words of this structure are always so accented, e.g. *ḏā́lika*.

Word juncture

Differences in the shape of a word may be entailed according to whether or not it is in immediate contact with another word. A word followed by a pause in utterance can be said to be in 'pre-pausal' position; one not preceded by another word, to be in 'post-pausal' position. Similarly, immediate contact with another word constitutes 'pre-juncture' or 'post-juncture' position. The actual incidence of pause is very variable. At one extreme, it may not occur until the end of the full sentence, or even paragraph; at the other, pre-pausal forms may be used in every word which is not in the very closest juncture. A normal midway use is exemplified in a sentence quoted by Monteil[2]: 'I shall speak to you today / on the topic of heroism / as it is depicted by the literature of Andalus / and of North Africa /'; the obliques mark the pauses, while the phrases between obliques are in juncture.

The effects of juncture operate on the beginning and the end of the word in diametrically opposite ways: in pre-juncture position or post-pausal position the word has phonetic elements which are not present in post-juncture or pre-pausal position.

The principal results of pre-pausal position are:

(i) final short vowels which are present in pre-juncture position do not appear in pre-pausal position, so that pre-juncture *baʿdu* contrasts with pre-pausal *baʿd*.

(ii) the syntactic morphemes *-un* and *-in* (p. 52) appear only in pre-juncture position, not in pre-pausal.

(iii) the syntactic morpheme *-an* of pre-juncture had in ancient Arabic a pre-pausal reflex *-ā*. SA normally retains this *-an* as a

[1] It is this feature, rather than detectable consonant length, which identifies such words. Although this would in itself suggest that the accent in such cases had phonemic value, I have been unable to discover any pair of words which would validate this; there is no word **máḥal*.

[2] *L'arabe moderne*, p. 317.

stable morpheme irrespective of position (particularly when it has adverbial function): *'ayḍan* 'also' is now so pronounced whether in pre-juncture or pre-pausal position. One might occasionally encounter pronunciations eliminating this morpheme in pre-pause (as with *-un* and *-in*), though this is, strictly speaking, a vernacular characteristic.

(iv) in some cases the termination *-in* is not purely a syntactic morpheme, but contributes also to the lexical identification of the word (pp. 52, vi); with these, the pre-pausal realization in SA is usually *-ī*, occasionally *-in.*[1]

(v) the *t* of the 'feminine' morpheme (p. 39) disappears in pre-pausal position along with the phonetic items mentioned above in (i) and (ii): pre-juncture *ssanatu, ssanati, sanatun, sanatin* all uniformly have the pre-pausal reflex *ssana/sana*. In the case of the *-an* mentioned in (iii), its treatment again largely depends on the syntactic value of the morpheme: adverbial *riyāḍatan* 'by way of exercise' would normally be retained in pre-pause, but *'išrūna sanatan* 'twenty years' *might* be realized before pause as *'išrūna sana*. In verse, however, the *t* appears in pre-pausal position as *-h*, at least to the extent that it rhymes with words where *h* is a different morpheme, e.g. the enclitic pronoun (p. 40), or a phoneme which is part of the structure of the lexical item: M. Nu'ayma, a modern Lebanese poet, rhymes *qiyāmah* 'resurrection' (pre-juncture *qiyāmati*) with *k̲itāmah* 'its end' (pre-juncture *k̲itāma-hu*).

The rules of verse, moreover, have always admitted, as an alternative to the elimination of a final short vowel, or of a short vowel + *-n*, the lengthening of the vowel. Nor has the elimination of such vowels ever been applicable to all words whatsoever: pre-juncture *'ana* 'I' had in ancient Arabic the pre-pausal reflex *'anā*, never **'an*. This is equally true of SA, and there are other words where SA does not admit elimination of the final short vowel, such as *lam yabqa* 'he did not remain'. It would be difficult to say, however, whether the vowel in such a case is lengthened, owing to the point mentioned, p. 20, about neutralization of final length phoneme.

[1] On this point I find myself in conflict with an otherwise wholly admirable description of SA, namely R. S. Harrell's 'Linguistic analysis of Egyptian radio Arabic' (in *Contributions to Arabic linguistics*, p. 36). There he refuses to pronounce on the point, on the grounds that words of this class are extremely rare in any event, and that in 200 pages of transcribed text he has not found a single example of one in pre-pausal position. This seems to be an unfortunate accident: it is difficult to believe that a news item does not sometimes end *lbaḥṯu jārī* 'the investigation is proceeding'. As a result, however, of this accident he goes on to surmise that a pronunciation *jār*, used in a broadcast, 'would probably be consciously noted and reacted to as "elegantly classical"'. I would go further than this and assert that this realization is not part of SA at all, and would be unintelligible in a broadcast since *jār* in SA would be interpreted as 'neighbour'.

The effects of post-pausal position are occasioned by the principles of syllabification (p. 20); a word beginning with two consonant phonemes is in SA non-viable in post-pausal position (or after a word ending in a consonant). In post-pausal position such a word is made viable by prefixing *hamz* + vowel; but this phonic feature is purely positionally determined and has no structural or morphemic function whatever. Words like *lmadā*, *ssawdā* and *jlis* are post-juncture forms which must be realized in post-pausal position as *'almadā*, *'assawdā* and *'ijlis*. In juncture with a preceding word ending in a consonant, a liaison vowel must be pronounced: *ʿan* + *lmadā* produces *ʿan i lmadā*. In either of these cases, the quality of the vowel employed varies according to somewhat elaborate rules, which are not detailed here.

3

THE SCRIPT

Arabic script has a genetic relationship with the Latin alphabet, since both are historically traceable back to a script current on the Levant coast around 1000 B.C. and used for the notation of the language which we call Old Phoenician. That script had a repertory of twenty-two symbols, all written individually (as in our print style as opposed to handwriting); and the values of the symbols were exclusively consonantal, the script showing no means of noting a vowel at all.

In the eighth century B.C., the same script was employed for the rendering of Old Aramaic, but with one seminal development, namely the use of a few of the symbols as vowel notation, though without losing their consonantal value, so that these symbols were henceforth ambiguous. A century or so later, the Greeks borrowed this script, but abandoned the consonantal values of the vowel letters, so that the Greek alphabet is classifiable into mutually exclusive groups of consonants and vowels. The Greek alphabet is the ancestor of modern European scripts.

About the same time also, a form of script was introduced into South Arabia which had close affinities with the Old Phoenician script, but which expanded the range of the alphabet to twenty-nine symbols with distinctive shapes, in order to cope with the phonemic consonantal repertory of the South Arabian language. Script forms closely analogous to this became widely prevalent throughout the south and centre of the Arabian peninsula, where they remained in normal use down to the fifth century A.D., but thereafter fell into disuse; and in the Horn of Africa, where they ultimately evolved into the Ethiopic script used for rendering present-day Amharic, etc.

Aramaic script evolved through many centuries without taking the step which the Greeks had, so that its facilities for vowel notation remained restricted. By the early centuries A.D. it developed into Syriac script, used for the dialect of the Near Eastern Christians, and into varieties used by the pagan kingdoms of Palmyra and Nabatene. Syriac, Palmyrene and Nabataean are all characterized by the fact that the custom had developed of linking many of the letters together within the boundaries of a single word by 'ligatures', as in our modern handwriting forms. This had two results, one being that certain letters, when occurring at the end of a word, came to have different shapes from those appearing elsewhere (just as in English down to the eighteenth century, *s* at the end of a word had a different shape from the 'long' ſ used otherwise). The other was that certain letters tended to lose their distinctive linear shapes and become ambiguous. In Syriac, the letters *d* and *r* became linearly indistinguishable, and were differentiated by the device of placing a dot under or over the letter. In Palmyrene and Nabataean this tendency was even more marked, but no attempt was made to obviate the confusion by the use of dots, and these scripts are therefore extremely difficult to interpret.

The script of the Nemara inscription (p. 13) is essentially a Nabataean one. It shows no notation at all for an open-quality vowel nor for any short vowel, but long *ū* and *ī* are marked by ambiguous letters serving also for the consonantal values *w* and *y*; length of a consonant is not marked at all; and it is still limited to the repertory of the Aramaic script, which is inadequate for the consonant phonemes of Arabic. Further ambiguities are occasioned by this: not only are several pairs of originally distinct letters now indistinguishable, but the *ḥ* symbol is also used for the notation of *k̲*, a phoneme for which Aramaic provided no distinctive notation.

Arabic script proper appears in the early seventh century, and is manifestly based on the same model as the Nemara script, sharing many of its characteristics. Sporadic attempts were made, however, to resolve the multiple ambiguities of the letter values by the use, as in Syriac, of dots: e.g. *j* was distinguished from *ḥ* by a dot under the letter, *k̲* by a dot over it. In this way an alphabet of twenty-eight letters developed, of which only six would be unambiguous if the device of dotting had not been adopted. These dots, although thus an integral part of the letter, remained somewhat sporadically used in early and medieval times.

It was not until the eighth century, when the Qur'ān was already extensively circulating in seventh century script, that a system was developed, designed to secure the correct reading of the Holy Book, by which short vowels were marked by symbols placed above or below the consonant which they follow in speech; other symbols placed above the letter marked absence of a following vowel, and length of a consonant. But these marks never came into general use, and to the present day the system is only used in texts of the Qur'ān, in grammar books and reading books for children, and to some extent in poetry. In the current script of today, short vowels and absence of vowel remain wholly unmarked, and even consonant length is only marked in more scholarly books, not in newspapers.

In the matter of long vowel notation, seventh-century script had evolved only a short way from the Nemara conventions, to the extent of sporadically using the letter *'alif* (Greek *alpha*), which in the older Semitic script systems had noted the consonant *hamz*, to note length of the open-quality vowel. Yet in a number of cases this notation was absent as it had been in the Nemara script. This feature of seventh-century script has survived in vestigial form to the present day, for there are some very commonly occurring words in which *ā* is not marked even now, e.g. the demonstrative *ḏālika* 'that', *Allāh*, etc. But apart from those words, the convention of marking *ā* by *'alif* has been, since the eighth century, universal.

The use of the originally consonantal *'alif* as a vowel notation has parallels in other Semitic scripts, notably Syriac. But there was another factor in the Arabic situation which facilitated the evolution, and it is one which has considerably affected the conventions of Arabic script to the present day: differences between the Meccan dialect of the early seventh century and the eastern Arabian dialects (p. 13). One item of those differences was that the consonantal *hamz* had ceased to be part of the phonemic repertory of the Meccan dialect, where the sound was not a phoneme but occurred only at the beginning of a word and conditioned by post-pausal position. There was therefore, in the orthography in which the Qur'ān was first written down, no use for a consonantal *'alif* except at the beginning of a word; in other positions, *hamz* had either been eliminated altogether, or had shifted to *w*, *y* or vowel length according to its phonetic context in the word. The eastern dialects on the other hand retained *hamz* as a fully functioning phoneme. The eighth-century grammarians of Lower Iraq, being in immediate contact with the eastern dialects, succeeded in imposing the eastern pronunciations as standard. But the prestige of the written Qur'ān was such that there could be no question of altering the accepted written text. The device was therefore adopted of marking the *hamz* phoneme by a symbol placed, like the short vowel marks, above or below the letter which, in the seventh-century orthography, had replaced it; in cases where the Meccan pronunciation had eliminated *hamz* altogether, the mark was written in isolation, but still apart from the level of the alphabetic letters. It is also placed above or below an initial *'alif*, although it might have been considered redundant here, seeing that a word cannot begin with a vowel (p. 20), and in fact some less conscientious typographers today do omit it in this position;

there is however a reason why its use is desirable, discussed below. The *hamz* notation is not regarded as a letter of the alphabet, in spite of the fact that in SA it notes an essential phoneme of the language.

A further manifestation of the Meccan versus eastern contrast lies in the fact that certain words in Meccan dialect were pronounced with a terminal *-ay*[1] where the eastern dialects had *-ā*. Here again, the eastern pronunciation has been imposed on SA, without any change in the ancient spelling convention. The present-day spelling *bky* represents the pronunciation */bakā/*.

Various other curiosities of orthographic convention of today are equally traceable to ancient Meccan practice. One of these is that in Quranic orthography, *w* at the end of a word was often followed by a conventional and wholly non-phonetic *'alif*; present-day practice has retained this feature, though restricting it to cases where the *w* marks the plural morpheme in a verb.

Another salient feature of script conventions is that the 'article' (p. 37), which is a morpheme realized sometimes as *l* and sometimes as consonantal length, is invariably noted as *l*, irrespective of the actual pronunciation.

Ancient orthography showed a general tendency towards spelling every word as if in isolation, thus reflecting both pre-pausal and post-pausal phenomena; the reader was left to supply the requisite juncture features. This is still the case today.

In consequence, the *-n* of the *-in* and *-un* terminations (p. 52) is not marked at all in the usual script, and in the full vowelling system only by a distinctive variety of the short-vowel mark[2]; and the *-an* termination is marked by *'alif*, reflecting the ancient pre-pausal realization *-ā*. The pre-pausal form of the feminine morpheme was marked by *-h*, and this was generally used in all positions; but Quranic orthography does contain sporadic instances where the pre-juncture form is phonetically spelt with *t*. Later usage has combined these two unsystematically used variants by adding two dots (characteristic of the letter *t*) to the *h*. The resulting symbol has to be evaluated according to the context: $s + n +$ dotted *h* is *sana* in pre-pausal position, *sanat-* plus appropriate vowel in pre-juncture.

Words of which the basic morphological shape begins with *cc* or *c̄* are spelt, both in post-juncture and post-pausal position, with an initial *'alif* reflecting the *hamz* required by post-pausal position. The

[1] Or at least some sound with a strong palatal quality which could be most appropriately noted by *y*, though its exact nature cannot now be defined.

[2] This applies both to the purely syntactic *-in* termination and to the *-in* with added lexical value mentioned on p. 22[1]. Consequently, the two examples there given, 'the investigation is continuing' and 'the investigation is a neighbour', are, in the normal unvowelled script, homographic.

full vowel-marking system does however distinguish between this merely positionally determined *hamz* and a fully functional one, to the extent that in post-juncture position of a word beginning with *cc* or *c̄* the *'alif* carries a special juncture mark, in lieu of the ordinary *hamz* mark.

Here too, present-day practice retains a vestigial trace of an ancient convention: the juncture *bi* + *smi* 'in the name of' is spelt phonetically as *bsm*, without *'alif*, when used in the phrase 'in the name of God' though not otherwise.

This observation leads on to another point, which is that Arabic script shows a repugnance to treating a phonetic segment consisting only of consonant + short vowel as a 'word'. Items such as *bi* 'in/by' and *wa* 'and', although by a structural analysis they are clearly independent words, are conventionally written as if part of the following word. And the enclitic pronouns (p. 40) are attached, irrespective of phonetic content, to the preceding word.

Transliteration

The rendering of Arabic in Latin script involves problems more acute than are normal in the case of most other non-Latin scripts. Even the primary need, of assigning Latin alphabet equivalents to the Arabic phonemes, has never been decisively met; there are some half-dozen competing systems in current use. All that one can do is to make an arbitrary choice between these systems, and the one I have chosen for this book is that employed in the English version of Wehr's dictionary.

Since however a dictionary cites words mainly in isolation, it does not encounter the additional problems posed in a work of the present nature by the juncture phenomena.

In principle, words or phrases divorced from a context will here be presented in pre-pausal form. Where, however, it is desirable to indicate what the pre-juncture form would be, the juncture element is presented in raised minuscule type.

It is worth while warning the reader that many European scholars omit ' at the beginning of the word in their transliteration, on the ground that an initial vowel is always necessarily preceded by *hamz*, and so they will write *iṭbāq*. Yet at the same time, they will, in the case of words beginning with *cc* or *c̄*, insert the vowel characteristic of post-pausal position, and write *istiqlāl*. These practices are undesirable for my purpose. In the first place, they obscure the difference between the *hamz* of *'iṭbāq* which is stable and functional, and the *hamz* which occurs in *'istiqlāl* only in post-pausal position: in post-juncture position the difference appears in that *wa* + *'iṭbāq* gives *wa-'iṭbāq*, but *wa* + *stiqlāl* gives *wa-stiqlāl*. Secondly, in post-juncture position of *cc-* and *c̄-* words, not only is the vowel which makes them viable that of the preceding word as in the example quoted above, but even when it is the liaison vowel used after a word terminating in a consonant, the quality of that vowel is determined by the previous word: *ʿan* + *stiqlāl* gives /*ʿan i stiqlāl*/, *hum* + *stiqlāl* gives /*hum u stiqlāl*/, etc. The liaison vowel is consequently best regarded as part of the preceding word in all cases. Words beginning with *cc*- or *c̄*- are hence here presented as such, though the reader must bear in mind that in post-pausal position they must be pronounced with an additional ʼ*v*-. In the quotation of phrases the liaison vowel will be marked by lowered minuscule.

The citation of a phrase divorced from its context demands a notation for the variable element dependent on the syntactic relationship to the total sentence, and this is noted by raised *v* when the variation embraces all three vowel qualities. Two-quality syntactic variations are noted by raised minuscules with / separating the possible variants.

Items joined together in the conventions of the script, but structurally separate words, are hyphenated.

4

THE WORD

In any language with a long literary tradition, and a script which conventionally isolates one speech-segment as a 'word', the consciousness of such a unit must have been present when the conventions of the script were first established, and a feedback from the process of learning to read and write in subsequent times has reinforced that consciousness. I do not propose, therefore, to speak about the identification of the 'word' as a segment of utterance, beyond the following few remarks.

In spite of script conventions (p. 28), it can be taken as certain that words such as the coordinating functional *wa* 'and', and the preposition *bi* 'in/by', are words in every sense. For they function in exactly the same way as the coordinating functional *ṯumma* 'and later' and the preposition *ʿalā* 'on', which have a larger phonetic bulk, and which are unquestionably words in Arabic linguistic feeling.

The status of certain pronoun items, conventionally written as part of the preceding word, is more debatable. Faced with the item *-ī* 'my', which is junctured to its substantive in such a way that its removal would not leave a viable word, a linguist might be inclined to register it as a morphemic variation of the substantive. But this item is anomalous, and all other such items could be deleted without impairing the viability of the preceding word. On the other hand, these pronouns are not themselves viable in isolation from the term with which they structurally associate. 'With John and Mary' is represented in Arabic by the same four words; but it is not possible to say 'with you and him' otherwise than by repeating the preposition 'with'. Moreover, if the speaker hesitates in the middle of a sentence, he can continue it as if no break had occurred provided that he resumes with any other kind of word than one of these pronoun items; if he wishes to resume with one of these, he must repeat the word preceding the break. Probably, therefore, one should regard these pronoun items as enclitics which must be in close juncture with the word with which they are structurally associated.

The establishment of word classes for any language can be undertaken on a morphological or a functional basis, or both. For Arabic it is necessary to take account of both. For example, verbs are principally identifiable as such by their morphological shape, since the functions which they embody can be performed by words other than verbs; while on the other hand the identification of words as adjectives is possible only on a functional basis, since their morphological structure is in no way distinctive.

Morphologically, one can make a primary classification between words which group into sets exhibiting morphological variations having either semantic or syntactic value, and those which have a stable morphological shape. To the first class belong verbs and nouns; to the second prepositions and functionals of coordination, subordination and modification (emphasis, negation, etc.). Pronouns and demonstratives rank properly with the first class, since they exhibit morphemic indications of gender, number, etc. But their morphological analysis is elaborate, and it is in practice easier to list them as if they were morphologically stable, than to attempt to describe them, as one can nouns and verbs, analytically.

Easily the most striking thing to a European language speaker who approaches Arabic is the morphological structure of nouns and verbs. An English word such as 'film' is a stable sequence of four phonemes in determined order; any additional morphemes, such as the plural morpheme in 'films', cannot disturb that nucleus of phonemes without making the word lose its recognizable identity. But in Arabic, verbs and nouns are a combination of two morphological strata: a sequence of consonant phonemes in determined order, commonly called the 'root', which is the prime lexical item; and a pattern of vowel (and sometimes consonant) phonemes into which the root consonants are slotted in determined positions. Both root and pattern are theoretical abstractions, and can only be actualized in combination with each other.

There are a large number of nouns in which three root consonants $R_1R_2R_3$ are inserted into the pattern *CiCC* characteristic of a singular noun, or into the pattern *'aCCāC* which is the matching plural morpheme. When the Arabs adopted 'film' as a loanword, they did not envisage the vowel as part of the lexical item 'film' but as part of the singular morpheme pattern: its Arabic plural is consequently *'aflām*. To take a native example, *muqātil* 'fighter' is analyzable as a combination of the morphological pattern $muR_1\bar{a}R_2iR_3$ and the consonantal root sequence *qtl*. In Arabic dictionaries, the entries for native Arabic nouns and verbs are alphabetically arranged according to the root consonants; so *muqātil* will be found under *q* and not *m*.

The two semivowels are capable of functioning as root consonants. But the application of morphological patterns to roots containing one or more of the semivowels will sometimes entail modification of the resulting structural pattern, including the possibility that the semi-vowel root consonant plus an adjacent vowel may disappear entirely in the ultimate shape of the word. These modifications are stateable in a set of somewhat elaborate rules,[1] and it will suffice here to give one or two examples:

$R_1aR_2aR_3a$ with root *bdw* yields not **badawa* but *badā*;
$yaR_1R_2uR_3u$ with root *kwn* yields not **yakwunu* but *yakūnu*;
$R_1aR_2iR_3tu$ with root *kyd* yields not **kayidtu* but *kidtu*;
$R_1aR_2aR_3at$ with root *bky* yields not **bakayat* but *bakat*;
$yaR_1R_2iR_3u$ with root *wrd* yields not **yawridu* but *yaridu*.

A further point in the application of pattern to root is that a root semivowel is in most cases replaced by ʼ when incorporated into a pattern in which it is the *R* in the sequence *-āRi-*, or in *-āR* at the end of the stem: $R_1\bar{a}R_2iR_3$ + *jwz* yields *jāʼiz* and not **jāwiz*, $\text{'}iR_1R_2\bar{a}R_3$ + *jry* yields *ʼijrāʼ* and not **ʼijrāy*.

These features constitute a major problem for beginners in Arabic, for the elucidation of the root of such a word, and hence the possibility of tracing it in the dictionary, is often difficult. On occasion, the phenomenon leads to homonymity: *zin* may mean 'weigh!' and is then attributable to root *wzn*, or 'adorn!' and is then attributable to *zyn*.

Roots with $R_2 = R_3$ also result in modifications of the word patterns into which they enter. A standard noun-plural pattern $\text{'}aR_1R_2iR_3a$ exemplified for root *sʼl* in *ʼasʼila* 'questions', when applied to root *dll* produces not **ʼadlila* but *ʼadilla* 'proofs'.

The great majority of Arabic roots have three consonants. Four-consonant roots are not too uncommon. But it is only substantives which exhibit two, or five plus, root consonants. In the three-consonant root, the occurring permutations of phonemes are limited by a law which has been formulated by J. H. Greenberg,[2] of which the following simplified version can be given:

(i) The semivowels lie outside the operation of the law.
(ii) roots with $R_1 = R_2$ are unknown, but $R_2 = R_3$ is very common.
(iii) the consonant phonemes must be divided into four groups, (a) the labials *bmf*, (b) 'liquids' *l n r*, (c) other linguals as listed on pp. 17–8,

[1] The most practical account of the rules is found in the chapters devoted to 'racines anormales' in R. Blachère's *Eléments d'arabe classique*.
[2] 'Patterning of root morphemes in Semitic' (*Word* 6, 1950, p. 178).

(d) the remaining consonants; and there is a marked tendency, subject to (ii) and to various exceptions detailed by Greenberg, for no root to contain more than one consonant from each group.

All Arabic verbs can be analysed on the root + pattern principle. But a handful of very ancient substantives contain only two consonants and are not capable of representation in terms of a normal word-pattern; for the purposes of evolving morphological variations of such words, they are treated as if they had an additional semivowel root consonant, so that *'ak̲* 'brother' is treated as if it belonged to root *'k̲w* in order to generate the plural of pattern $R_1iR_2R_3\bar{a}n$ namely *'ik̲wān* 'brothers'.

Loanwords naturally also resist analysis on the root + pattern basis, unless they happen accidentally to resemble (as with 'film') a known Arabic pattern. Even granted this, however, they require (being almost entirely substantives) a machinery for generating plurals, and a widespread device is to isolate four consonants from the word and apply them to one of the plural patterns $R_1aR_2\bar{a}R_3iR_4$ or $R_1aR_2\bar{a}R_3iR_4a$: *'usquf* 'bishop' (from Greek *episkopos*) has the plural *'asāqifa*.[1]

The classification of words on a functional plane will be discussed in the following chapters.

[1] This can lead to somewhat bizarre results: it is far from easy to devine that *hatālira wa-masālina* means 'Hitlers and Mussolinis'.

5

ENTITY TERMS: I

It has been held by some linguists that every statement contains as minimal elements a topic, or 'theme', about which the statement is made, and a 'predicate' or communication about the theme. In 'the new shoes which I'm wearing hurt me', the words 'hurt me' constitute the predicate stated about the theme 'the new shoes which I'm wearing'.

This doctrine has certainly pragmatical usefulness for Arabic, inasmuch that any speech segment which is potentially capable of functioning as a theme belongs to a functional class to which I apply the designation 'entity term'. The entity term may be a single word, or a word plus amplificatory items (such as 'new' and 'which I'm wearing' in the above example). Words classifiable as entity terms subdivide into substantives, pronouns and demonstratives. In addition, a clause structure, if suitably marked, can assume the function of a substantive in the sentence, and then becomes eligible to be ranked as an entity term, although the actual employment of such a clause as a theme may entail some modifications of its structure (p. 92).

I must here stress a terminological point: since substantives and adjectives are distinguishable only by function, not by morphological shape, it may be impossible when quoting a word out of context to assert that it is either one or the other, this being determinable only by the syntactic context. I am therefore obliged at times to use the expression 'noun' to cover both substantives and adjectives. Some nouns function exclusively as substantives, a very large number function either as substantive or adjective; but no nouns function exclusively as adjectives. It is impossible without a sentence context to determine whether *ʿādil* represents the English adjective 'just' or a substantive = 'a just man'.

Nouns, pronouns and demonstratives incorporate concepts of number, gender and 'definition' versus 'indefinition' (pp. 36–7). Nouns and demonstratives also have to a partial extent morphemic marking of their syntactic function in relation to the total sentence; in pronouns this marking is effected by the choice of one out of several sets of pronoun items.

Verbal abstract

This is a type of substantive denoting in principle the concept common to all the morphological variations of a verb, abstracted from those elements in the verb which show how the concept is actualized in experience. In practice, however, an Arabic word-pattern recognizable as a verbal abstract covers a wide semantic spectrum. *wuṣūl* covers both the pure abstraction represented by English 'to arrive' as in 'to travel hopefully is better than to arrive', and 'arrival'; it also subsumes, as indeed does 'arrival', both 'the fact of arriving/having arrived' and 'the idea/possibility of arriving'. In many instances, the spectrum extends into the concrete. This is a phenomenon visible in English, where for instance 'donation' may represent 'act of donating' as in 'their donation was a gracious gesture', or the concrete 'thing donated' as in 'their donation was ten shillings'; in Arabic, *rizq* is not only applicable to the abstract 'act/notion of providing someone with his daily needs' but also to the concrete 'wages'.

Morphologically, the verbal abstracts which match primary verbs have unpredictable word-patterns, and constitute lexical items. But a secondary verb-stem (p. 72) has a single predictable word-pattern for its matching verbal abstract.

Participles

The participle is a noun (substantive or adjective) which, like the verbal abstract, matches a verb. Morphologically, it has a wholly predictable word-pattern in relation to a verb of any type. The fundamental semantic value of a participle is that of describing an entity about which the verb can be predicated and nothing more: substantivally used, the participle matching 'he writes' connotes 'person who writes' or 'writer'; adjectivally used, the participle matching 'he hangs' might appear in a phrase like 'a hanging judge'. There is however one remarkable structural elaboration of participle use which will be discussed later (p. 94).

Like the verbal abstract, the participle is capable of considerable semantic extension. Many words which have the pattern of a participle contain highly specialized senses within their semantic spectrum, in addition to the fundamental value. The reader faced with a participle pattern will always need to consider whether in the given context it is being used in the fundamental value or in one of the specialized meanings: *qāṭiʿ* has not only the generalized sense of 'someone who/something which cuts' (or, used adjectivally, 'trenchant') but also the specialized meanings 'secant (in geometry)' and 'screen'.

Derivational nouns

In ancient Arabic, a morpheme *-iyy* added after the stem of a substantive was used to connote tribal and geographical affiliation: *tamīmiyy* 'a member of the Tamim tribe', *ḥijāziyy* 'belonging to Hijaz' (substantivally or adjectivally). In the eighth century, the intellectual explosion demanded the creation of a large number of relational terms, and this morpheme became very widely used to denote relationship, in the broadest sense, with the basic substantive: *malik* 'king' generates *malikiyy* 'royal'. The feminine form of the morpheme, *-iyya*, was also put to use for coining the many abstracts which came to be needed: *ʿaql* 'mind/intelligence' generates *ʿaqliyy* '(something) mental/intellectual' and *ʿaqliyya* 'mentality/intellect'. There are even one or two cases of the morpheme being applied to a word other than a substantive: 'modality/manner' is expressed by *kayfiyya* ⟨howness⟩ based on *kayf*[a] 'how?'.

In SA both morphemes are extremely productive and are capable of furnishing neologisms as required: e.g. *šuyūʿiyy* 'communist' (both substantive and adjective), *šuyūʿiyya* 'communism'; and *-iyy* is universally used for national affiliations, *'inkilīziyy* 'English/Englishman'. They have, however, the disadvantage, arising out of their extensive use, of ambiguity, for they are the sole means of rendering a variety of English formations: *wāqiʿiyya* is both 'reality' and 'realism', *'imbarāṭūriyya* is both 'empire' and 'imperialism'.

The attachment of *-iyy(a)* to a verbal abstract can point a contrast in second-degree abstraction with the first-degree abstraction of the basic word, and with the matching participle: *wujūd* 'existence' has a matching participle *mawjūd* 'existent', but has generated *wujūdiyy* 'existential/existentialist' and *wujūdiyya* 'existentialism'; *'intāj* 'production' has the matching participle *muntij* 'producer' but has generated *'intājiyy* 'productive' and *'intājiyya* 'productivity'; *stiʿmār* 'colonization', *mustaʿmir* 'colonist', *stiʿmāriyy* 'colonial', *stiʿmāriyya* 'colonialism'.

Definition

Pronouns and demonstratives are allusive, but unambiguous inasmuch as the hearer is expected to be able to identify the entity alluded to by the speaker. Lack of ambiguity also characterized substantives which are applicable only to a single, unique entity, such as 'Baghdad' and 'Tamburlain'. The unambiguous quality of all these is what is here referred to as 'definition': all such words are 'defined' by their own nature.

Another kind of substantive is applicable to any one or more individual members of a category, such as 'village'. Substantives of this kind can appear in several types of context. Where the context is such that it establishes without ambiguity the individuality of the substantive within its category, English uses the functional marker 'the', as in 'at nightfall we reached the village', a statement only intelligible if the hearer can from contextual considerations identify what particular village is meant. This constitutes 'particularized' definition, and the Arabic marker is a morpheme with positionally determined varieties: lengthening of the initial consonant where this is a lingual (*ssana* 'the year'), a prefixed *l* if the initial consonant is anything else (*lqarya* 'the village'); in the case of a word which already begins with *cc* or *c̄*, the *l* must be prefixed to the post-pausal form (*ttiḥād* 'union' has the post-pausal form *'ittiḥād*, hence *l'ittiḥād* 'the union').

In a second type of situation, the precise identity of the substantive within its category is irrelevant, inasmuch as the speaker is interested only in assigning the entity or group of entities to its/their category, not in individualizing it. The English marker in this case is 'a' in the singular contrasting with 'some' in the plural: 'we reached a village', 'we reached some villages'. A substantive of this kind is in Arabic an unmarked term contrasting with the term marked by the morpheme described above: *sana* 'a year', *qarya* 'a village', *qurā* 'some villages'. It is therefore possible to refer to the Arabic marked-term morpheme simply as '*the* article', since it contrasts with zero and not with some other morpheme.

But irrelevancy of individualization may also arise from the speaker's intending his utterance to apply to every individual, or group of individuals, in the category. English marks this situation by singular 'a' contrasting with plural zero: 'a village is always full of gossip', 'villages are always full of gossip'. In Arabic this situation is marked by the article.

The Arabic article consequently has two distinct functions: the particularizing one, and the generalizing one just described. Whereas the English contrast between 'a' and 'the' is a contrast in the relevancy of individualization, the Arabic contrast between the article and zero marking is one of unambiguousness versus ambiguousness. On hearing 'we reached a village' the hearer might wish to seek for further clarification and ask 'What village was it?', but he could not do so reasonably if confronted with either of the unambiguous statements 'we reached the village' or 'a village is always full of gossip'. Definition for Arabic is the quality of lacking ambiguousness, whether that be occasioned by the inherent nature of the entity term or by the use of the article in either of its functional values. Grammatically, the results of definition are the same, no matter how it arises, in nearly all cases.

On occasion, undefined status accompanies a heightening of the numerical contrast between singular and plural: singular *qarya* versus plural *qurā* may mark not only the contrast between 'a village' and 'some villages', but also the contrast between 'one village' and 'several villages'.

There is a class of substantives which can be envisaged either as a category embracing a multiplicity of members, or as an indivisible entity, such as 'sorrow' and 'devaluation'. These in English take 'a' or 'the', and in Arabic zero marking or the article, if envisaged in the former way, as in 'he experienced a deep sorrow' and 'the devaluation which took place last year was disastrous'. If envisaged as indivisible entities, they have zero marking in English, as in 'sorrow follows joy' and 'devaluation is a stupid policy'; in Arabic they are normally marked by the generalizing article in this case, but the undefined term does occur in some syntactic contexts (e.g. 'he is a man of sorrow').

It is convenient here to refer cursorily (see further pp. 44–5) to the fact that an adjective which amplifies a defined substantive must itself be marked by the article.

Number and gender

Numerical status in SA is tripartite: singularity; duality, alluding to two individuals; and plurality, which always implies more-than-duality.

In substantives, numerical status is marked by an extension of the word-stem in the case of duals and of one type of plural, which can therefore be called 'external'; the contrast in such cases is between an unmarked singular and marked dual and plural, as in *mujrim* 'a/one criminal' contrasting with the marked terms *mujrim*$^{\bar{a}/ay}$*n*^{i} 'two criminals' and *mujrim*$^{\bar{u}/\bar{\imath}}$*n*^{a} 'several criminals'. In another type of plural, conveniently called 'internal', the singular versus plural contrast is marked by two contrasting word-patterns, as in *jirm* 'body' contrasting with *ʼajrām* 'bodies'.

Internal plural patterns show great variety, and perhaps the only type worth special notice is the group *CaCāCiC*, *CaCāCīC* and *CaCāCiCa* (the last mainly used in substantives denoting persons). This group of patterns is applicable both to roots with four consonants and to nouns with a stem consisting of three root consonants plus an additional, non-root, consonant. Thus *ḵandaq* 'ditch' has plural *ḵanādiq*, with the four-consonant root *ḵndq*, and also *masjid* 'mosque' has plural *masājid*, with root *sjd* plus the non-root consonant *m*. In these patterns, the concept of a consonant additional to the root is frequently extended to cover the phoneme of vowel length, this being treated for the purpose of constructing a plural as if it resulted from a semivowel root consonant (p. 32): *fāris* 'cavalier' has plural *fawāris*, and *ʿarūs* 'bride' has plural *ʿarāʾis* (ibid).

Every substantive has a grammatical gender, masculine or feminine; though there are a few instances of common gender, i.e. the potentiality of treating the word as masculine or feminine at the speaker's discretion. Male persons are always grammatically masculine, females feminine, but non-persons may be either, and the only certain way of determining the gender of a substantive describing a non-person is by the nature of a pronoun which refers to it. There is indeed a morpheme so widely characteristic of feminines that the Arab grammarians call it the 'feminine marker', yet not every feminine substantive is so marked, nor does possession of the mark guarantee the femininity of the substantive (it is found in a few words denoting male persons, which are necessarily masculine).

This so-called 'feminine' marker is added after the word-stem and is, in the singular *-a* in pre-pausal position, *-at*^{v} in pre-juncture position. In the dual, *-at-* serves as a stem base for the addition of the dual morpheme described above. The external feminine plural morpheme is *-āt*^{v}.

The external masculine plural morpheme is used only for male persons. A masculine substantive denoting a non-person, unless it has an internal plural pattern, must use the external feminine plural marker: *bāṣ* 'bus' has plural *bāṣāt*.

In addition to the external feminine markers, there are two distinctive word-patterns which constitute internal marks of femininity (using external and internal in a sense similar to the way they have been used in connection with number markers), namely $R_1uR_2R_3\bar{a}$ and $R_1aR_2R_3\bar{a}$ʾ. These are singular patterns; the plural patterns which match them show some variety.

Nouns functioning adjectivally have the same morphemic markers of gender and number as those functioning substantivally.

Pronouns

Pronouns are substitutes for overt entity terms, and their use is largely conditioned by the ability of the hearer to identify the overt entity term to which they allude. They incorporate gender and number differentiations matching those of the entity terms to which they refer; but it is a striking feature of the SA gender and number system that pluralities of non-persons, whether masculine or feminine, are referred to by feminine singular pronouns.

Arabic pronouns comprise four sets, each consisting of twelve items:

(i) an item alluding to the speaker;

(ii) an item alluding to the speaker plus another or other persons;

(iii) two items alluding to one person addressed, distinguishing between male and female;

(iv) an item alluding to two persons addressed, with no gender distinction;

(v) two items alluding to a plurality of persons addressed, distinguishing male and female;

(vi) five items alluding to entities other than speaker or person(s) addressed, distinguishing between singular, dual and plural; and with gender distinction in singular and plural but not in the dual.

One set is 'independent' both in the functional sense and in being wholly independent words. Easily the commonest use of this set is in the function of a theme, but it can also be used to give extra emphasis to a preceding pronoun belonging to one of the other sets.

The second set are enclitics (pp. 30–1) attached to a verb, functioning as direct object thereto ('me', 'him', etc.); or to a substantive, functioning as amplifier of it ('my', 'his', etc.); or to a preposition. Morphologically, the first two of these functions are distinguished only in the item referring to the single speaker, which is *-nī* after a verb and *-ī* after a substantive; the combinations of preposition + pronoun produce certain morphological anomalies, though by and large the pronoun shows the same form as after a substantive.

The items in the two sets so far mentioned are schematically disposed as follows (independent set items first, enclitic second):

<table>
<tr><td rowspan="2"></td><td rowspan="2">speaker(s)</td><td rowspan="2">person(s) addressed</td><td colspan="2">other entities</td></tr>
<tr><td>person</td><td>non-person</td></tr>
<tr><td rowspan="2">sing.</td><td rowspan="2">*'ana*[1], *-nī*, *-ī*</td><td>masc. *'anta*, *-k*^{a}</td><td colspan="2">masc. *huwa*, *-h*^{u}</td></tr>
<tr><td>fem. *'anti*, *-k*^{i}</td><td colspan="2">fem. *hiya*, *-hā*</td></tr>
<tr><td rowspan="2">plur.</td><td rowspan="3">*naḥnu*, *-nā*</td><td>masc. *'antum*, *-kum*</td><td>masc. *hum*, *-hum*</td><td rowspan="2"></td></tr>
<tr><td>fem. *'antunna*, *-kunna*</td><td>fem. *hunna*, *-hunna*</td></tr>
<tr><td>dual</td><td>*'antumā*, *-kumā*</td><td colspan="2">*humā*, *-humā*</td></tr>
</table>

There are some positionally determined variants of the enclitic pronouns. The item *-ī* is replaced by *-ya* immediately after a long vowel or unlengthened semivowel (*'ayn-ī* 'my eye', *'aduww-ī* 'my enemy' versus *'aynā-ya* and *'aynay-ya* 'my eyes'). In *-hu*, *-hum*,

[1] Spelt *'anā*, see p. 22 (and p. 27 on 'isolation' orthography).

-hunna, *-humā* the vowel-quality *u* changes to *i* when *i* or *y* immediately precedes: *maʿnā-hum* 'their meaning' contrasts with *maʿānī-him* 'their meanings'. In verse, the *-hu*/*-hi* item commonly (though exceptions do occur) has a long vowel unless *v̄* immediately precedes, so that *bi-hī* contrasts with *fī-hi*.

The third and fourth pronoun sets function as agents of a verb, and are morphologically incorporated into the verb structure; they will therefore be described in Chapter 10.

In principle, a pronoun always refers to a previously mentioned overt entity, but there are two usages of pronouns which lie outside the operation of the principle. In one of these, the pronoun applicable to a plurality of males can be used non-specifically alluding to 'people in general', exactly as in the English usage 'They (i.e. people) say it will rain tomorrow'. Secondly, the pronoun applicable to a single masculine entity can be used in allusion to some fact or idea that has been mentioned, without there being any specific entity term to which it could be said to allude, as in 'he isn't coming today, and it is a great pity'.

This last usage lies at the basis of a further phenomenon, the use of this pronoun to foreshadow an entity term occurring later in the sentence, as in 'it's a great pity that he isn't coming today', where the logical theme of the predicate 'is a pity' is 'that he isn't coming'. The subsequent entity term can then (as the Arab grammarians express it) be said to 'explain' the pronoun. It is not however actually alluded to by the pronoun, for there are cases, common in Arabic but not capable of illustration in English, where the foreshadowing masculine singular pronoun is explained by a subsequent feminine or plural entity term. This occurs in contexts where, on the one hand, the sentence structure requires an entity term at the beginning of the sentence and, on the other hand, the logical theme is of such a nature that it cannot conveniently be placed first. In 'he declared that many authors who are indifferent to the demands of style write this', the functional 'that' requires to be followed by an entity term (p. 56), yet to place the lengthy logical theme 'many authors who are indifferent to the demands of style' in front of the succinct predicate 'write this' is rhythmically objectionable to the Arab ear (p. 109); such a sentence is therefore structured as ⟨he declared that-it, write this many authors, etc. . . .⟩.

Apart from the case of the foreshadowing pronoun, a fairly strong objection is felt to placing a pronoun before the overt term to which it alludes. The commonplace English structure 'As soon as he had ascended the throne, Henry discarded his former companions' is avoided in favour of 'Henry, as soon as he had ascended the throne, discarded . . .' or 'As soon as Henry had ascended the throne, he discarded . . .' This principle, combined with the requirement that a direct object pronoun must be enclitically attached to the verb (p. 40), has a notable effect on sentences where the verb is placed first (p. 63), if the agent of the verb in any way belongs to its direct object, as in 'the boy's uncle loved him': if it is desired to place the verb first in this sentence, it cannot be structured as *⟨loved-him the boy's uncle⟩ which would place the pronoun before the term to which it alludes, and it can only be structured as ⟨loved the boy his-uncle⟩. The principle is only infringed in a very few cases: in 'when the commission which was appointed to investigate the case had begun its work', the functional *lammā* 'when' requires an immediately following verb, yet the rhythmical principle mentioned above excludes placing 'its work' at the end of the sentence, and the structure ⟨when had begun its work the commission which . . .⟩ is unavoidable.

Demonstratives

The ordinary demonstrative resembles the pronoun in being allusive, and requiring a context to make the allusion understandable. But, also like a pronoun, the allusion can be to a generalized fact or idea that has been mentioned, and not to an overt entity.

Arabic has two sets of these demonstratives, corresponding to the English 'nearer' demonstratives, 'this, these' and the 'remoter' demonstratives 'that, those'. Each set comprises five items, distributed in a manner slightly different from pronouns, inasmuch as the gender contrast is here marked in the dual but not in the plural, thus (the 'nearer' item mentioned first):

		person	non-person
sing.	masc.	*hāḏā*: *ḏālik*^{a}	
	fem.	*hāḏihi*: *tilk*^{a}	
plur.	masc. & fem.	*hā'ulā'*^{i}: *'ulā'ik*^{a}	
dual	masc.	*hāḏ*$^{\bar{a}/ay}$*n*^{i}: *ḏ*$^{\bar{a}/ay}$*nik*^{a}	
	fem.	*hāt*$^{\bar{a}/ay}$*n*^{i}: *t*$^{\bar{a}/ay}$*nik*^{a}	

Demonstratives are defined entity terms, and capable of functioning without any amplification, as in 'I like this'. But whereas pronouns are regarded as wholly unambiguous and therefore incapable of being amplified,[1] demonstratives can be amplified by an explicit substantive. This corresponds to the English adjectival use of a demonstrative, as in 'I like this book', but the manner in which the Arabic demonstrative is used precludes us from regarding it as an adjective: it and the substantive have a parity of status reflected in the fact that it sometimes precedes and sometimes follows the entity term which explains it.

The requirement of parity of status entails that the explanatory substantive must be, like the demonstrative itself, defined. In so far as definition of the substantive is marked by the attachment of the article to that substantive, the demonstrative precedes it: *hāḏā lkitāb* ⟨this thing, the book⟩ 'this book'. In any other case, the demonstrative comes at the end of the total phrase; thus, if the substantive is inherently defined, *mūsā hāḏā* 'this Moses'. A substantive can also acquire defined status from a following entity term which amplifies it (p. 46), as with *maʿnā lkitāb* 'the meaning of the book', and in this case too, since *maʿnā* 'meaning' does not itself have its defined status marked by the article (but by the subsequent term), the demonstrative which has parity of status with *maʿnā* follows the full phrase, *maʿnā lkitāb hāḏā* 'this meaning of the book'. Other permutations of word order are possible, but all have different senses from those detailed above: they are either phrases in which the demonstrative does not have parity of status with the head word in the phrase, as in *maʿnā hāḏā* 'the meaning of this', and *maʿnā hāḏā lkitāb* 'the meaning of this book'; or predicative structures (pp. 67–8), as in *hāḏā mūsā* 'this is Moses', and *hāḏā maʿnā lkitāb* 'this is the meaning of the book'.

Beside the ordinary allusive demonstratives, there is another type of entity term which is also essentially demonstrative in nature, but depends for its intelligibility not on its allusion to an entity already known to the hearer, but on its being amplified by a subsequent clause. 'That is false' is intelligible in so far as the hearer has already the means of identifying the entity to which 'that' alludes. But 'that which you say is false' is only intelligible by virtue of 'that' being amplified by the clause structure 'which you say'. Entity terms which are unintelligible without an amplification of this nature have distinctive shapes in Arabic, and are discussed more fully later, under the heading of adjectival clauses, pp. 49–50.

[1] Structures such as *naḥnu lmuslimūn* 'we Muslims' do occur in SA, but seem to me best regarded as appositional structures with parity of status between the two terms; at all events, the status of *lmuslimūn* there is clearly different from its adjectival amplificatory status in *lmulūk*^{v} *lmuslim*$^{\bar{u}/\bar{\imath}}$*n* 'the Muslim kings'.

6

AMPLIFICATION OF SUBSTANTIVES

In so far as a single word is inadequate to describe the entity which the speaker has in mind, it can be amplified by one or more of the following: an adjective, another entity term, a prepositional phrase, or an amplifying (adjectival) clause structure.

In SA prose, all amplifications are placed immediately after the substantive which they amplify, and their relative order when more than one type of amplification is used is normally: amplified substantive → amplifying entity term → adjective → prepositional phrase → clause. This placing is, however, far from rigid in the case of the amplifying prepositional phrase, which can occur in front of the adjective, and even on occasion precede the amplified substantive: 'a violent desire for this' can be structured as ⟨a desire violent for this⟩ or ⟨a desire for this, violent⟩ and 'a desire for this' can be structured as ⟨for this a desire⟩.

Adjectives

It has already been said (p. 31) that one cannot establish for Arabic a word-class of adjectives, syntactic considerations being the only identificatory criterion of an adjective. There is a probability that in the most primitive stage of the language, the relationship between two terms which later came to be felt as one between substantive and adjective, was envisaged in a different way, namely as a coordination of two substantives with parity of status, comparable with what in European grammar would be termed an appositional relationship, as in 'William the conqueror' (though unlike the looser type of apposition expressed by 'William, a conqueror'). 'The just judge' would then have had to be evalued as 'the judge, the just man'.

A pointer to this conclusion is the rule, still valid in SA, that a word functioning as an adjective must exhibit the overt mark of defined versus undefined contrast corresponding to the status of the amplified substantive in that respect. The phrase *lqāḍī lʿādil* is recognizable as a substantive + adjective nexus, 'the just judge', by the presence of the article with the adjective as well as with the substantive; without this, the phrase would have a different value.

Another pointer in the same direction is that in ancient Arabic, the further one goes back, the more instances one can find where the term which later feeling would identify as an adjective is not gender-differentiated to match the gender of the 'substantive'; the 'adjectival' term *baʿīd*, without gender differentiation, would therefore in ancient times have to be evaluated as an appositional 'a remote thing' (retaining its own inherent gender status) rather than the adjective 'remote'. But from quite early times down to the present, it has become a rule that the adjective must be marked as masculine or feminine correspondingly to the grammatical gender of the substantive. The type of marking is characteristic of the word as such; so that an 'internally' marked feminine substantive may have an 'externally' marked adjective and vice versa; and an inherently feminine substantive with no overt mark of femininity will have an overtly marked adjective, as in *ḥarb bağīḍa* 'a detestable war' (*ḥarb* is grammatically feminine though not so marked). Equally, an inherently masculine substantive, even if formally marked 'feminine' (p. 39), is accompanied by an adjective without feminine marking: *k̲alīfa bağīḍ* 'a detestable caliph'.

In respect of numerical marking also, the adjective exhibits the same marker as its substantive, but with the proviso that pluralities of non-persons are not amplified by an adjective marked by the external plural morphemes, in lieu of which the feminine singular marker is used (as is the case with pronouns, see p. 39). On the other hand, an internal plural marker of the adjective is legitimate in all cases, whether the substantive denotes persons or non-persons, provided that the adjective has the morphological potentiality of internal plural marking. One has therefore the alternatives of *waqāʾiʿ ʿaẓīma* (adjective marked feminine singular) and *waqāʾiʿ ʿiẓām* (adjective with internal plural marking) 'mighty events'.

The annexion structure

The link between a noun and an entity term which amplifies it is termed by the Arab grammarians *ʾiḍāfa* 'annexion', and the noun thus amplified is said to be *muḍāf* 'annexed'. In default of any common European technicality connoting 'a noun amplified by an entity term'[1], I have felt obliged to retain the Arabic terminology, though it must be strongly emphasized that the 'annexed' term is the amplified one and

[1] Semitists will, however, recognize that this is what they have been accustomed to call a 'construct'.

not, as a European reader might *prima facie* suppose, the amplifying one.

In order to comprehend the Arabic annexion structure, it is best to regard it as parallel to the English form in which two nouns are juxtaposed, as in 'steam train', 'village doctor', 'orange peel'; the only difference lies in the relative placing of the two terms, for in Arabic the one which actually defines the entity meant (train, doctor, peel) comes first. The semantic implications of the structure are as open-ended in Arabic as in English ('steam train' is one powered by steam, 'village doctor' one who works in a village, 'orange peel' the peel which surrounds an orange); but it also subsumes English 'genitive' structures such as 'a village's doctor', 'the peel of an orange'. The significance of the parallel with the English 'village doctor' structure is that, as in English in that structure, the two terms are in closest juncture and cannot be separated, whereas they can be separated in the English genitive structures 'the village's new doctor', 'the peel, so brightly coloured, of an orange'; and further, that a single mark of definition or indefinition serves to mark the definitional status of the total phrase—'a village doctor' versus 'the village doctor'. In Arabic it is the amplifying term whose definitional status yields the definitional status of the whole phrase: consequently, an annexed substantive will not itself have the article. 'The tusk of an elephant' has in Arabic no element of definition about it, because it must be regarded as equivalent to 'an elephant tusk'. It follows, of course, that English expressions of the type 'a tusk of the elephant' cannot be represented by an Arabic annexion structure. When the amplifying term is inherently defined, this alone serves to give defined value to the whole phrase: *maʿnā hāḏā* 'the meaning of this'.

In spite of the semantic polyvalency of the annexion structure, nearly all its effective values can be classified under six broad headings, five of which are as follows (in all these five cases the annexed term is necessarily a substantive):

(i) relationship of identity between the two terms, as with 'London town', 'the village of Garsington', 'Albion's land'.

(ii) partitive relationship, where the annexed term is a part of the amplifying one, as in 'the majority of Englishmen', 'the poets of the Arabs'.

(iii) possessive relationship, taken in a very broad sense, as in 'the king's palace', 'the meaning of this'.

(iv) agent relationship, where the annexed term is a verbal abstract or participle matching a verb to which the amplifying term would function as agent, as in 'the death of Queen Victoria' matching 'Queen Victoria died'.

(v) object relationship, where the annexed term matches a verb to which the amplifying term would function as direct object, as in 'the assassination of President Kennedy' matching 'somebody assassinated President Kennedy'.

The significance of this classification lies in the fact that an annexion structure can be replaced by a prepositional amplifier, and the preposition used differs according to the type of relationship involved: identifying, partitive or agent annexion is replaced by the preposition *min*, possessive or object annexion by *li*. The annexion structure *hawā lfatā* 'the love of the boy' is replaceable by *lhawā min$_a$ lfatā* if it means 'the love which the boy feels', by *lhawā li-lfatā* if it means 'the love felt towards the boy'. Use of possessive *li* is however tending in SA to encroach on *min*: it is now natural to write *nniṣf^v l'awwal^v li-hāḏā l-qarn* 'the first half of this century'.

The principle that an annexed substantive in these structures cannot bear the article is important in distinguishing the annexion structure from a structure of substantive + adjective: *lmuġannī lmuʿammā* 'the blind minstrel' versus *muġannī lmuʿammā* 'the blind man's minstrel' (cf. p. 45).

There is, however, a characteristic Arabic idiom in which what we should naturally regard as a substantive + adjective relationship is represented in Arabic by two substantives in identificatory annexion: 'the great poets' being represented by *kibār^v ššuʿarā'* ⟨the great ones of [= who are] poets⟩.[1]

In the sixth type of annexion, the function of the amplifying term is to limit the sphere of applicability of the annexed term. Most writers have described this as a case where the annexed term is an adjective, but although this is statistically in SA the most common case,[2] it is by no means necessarily so; the adjectival function of an annexion phrase of this kind is simply an aftergrowth of the substantival function, as with adjectives in general (p. 44). *ṭawīl* can function as a substantive, 'a tall person/a long thing', as well as adjectivally 'tall/long', and it can be annexed in either case to a term limiting its relevance to a particular feature such as 'hair'. The resulting phrase can then be used either substantivally meaning ⟨a person long of hair⟩ 'a long-haired person', or adjectivally to amplify a preceding substantive such as 'youth' in 'a long-haired youth'.

An important structural difference between this type of annexion and the ones previously mentioned is that in limiting annexion the

[1] The reader may object that this relationship could be regarded as partitive, but examples culled from poetry (where this structure is particularly favoured) show that this is not so: 'deaf things of stones' does not imply that some stones hear, whereas 'the poets of the Arabs' does imply that some Arabs are not poets.

[2] For this reason, I have so described it myself in *Written Arabic*, §1:19.

limiting term is always marked as defined, but does *not* thereby make the total phrase defined, and the article *is* used with the annexed term if required: *ṭawīl*^v^ *ššaʿr* 'a long-haired person' contrasts with *ṭṭawīl*^v^ *ššaʿr* 'the long-haired person'.

Limiting annexion is much commoner in SA than a European would anticipate, and is often used to render other kinds of English structure, such as ⟨a policy short of term⟩ 'a short-term policy', ⟨a factor extreme of effect⟩ 'a highly effective factor'.

Joint annexion of two nouns linked by 'and' is a phenomenon which is rapidly gaining ground in SA, and it is now not uncommon to encounter structures such as 'beginning and end of the matter'. Traditionally minded writers still, however, tend to avoid this: for it nullifies the very close juncture felt to be necessary between annexed and amplifying terms, inasmuch as in such a structure the first term is followed immediately by 'and' instead of by an amplifying term as an annexed noun should be. The traditional structure for such a phrase is ⟨the beginnning of the matter and its end⟩.

Annexion structures which have become clichés are showing a slight tendency (albeit on a very minimal scale as yet) towards evolving into compound words. *raʾs māl* ⟨head of money⟩ 'capital' still receives from a writer in the literary tradition the defined form *raʾs*^v^ *lmāl*, though a writer less careful of the literary tradition might use the vernacular *rraʾs-māl.* But even the most traditionally minded writer cannot avoid using the compound form as base for the derivational nouns *raʾsmāliyy* 'capitalist' (substantive and adjective) and *rraʾs-māliyya* capitalism'.[1] Similarly *ssikkat*^v^ *lḥadīd* 'the railway' is tending to gain ground at the expense of the original coinage *sikkat*^v^ *lḥadīd* ⟨the way of iron⟩.

Prepositional amplification

Amplification of a noun by means of a prepositional phrase is common when either (i) this replaces an annexion structure (p. 47), so that *X hāḏā* 'the X of this' contrasts with *X li-hāḏā* 'an X of this'; or (ii) the amplified noun has a manifest semantic connection with a verbal concept, as is the case with participles and verbal abstracts in particular, but also with other words than those whose word-pattern is so classifiable (e.g. the derivational *masʾūliyya* 'responsibility' which is patently related to the verb meaning 'to question', see p. 115).

[1] It will be observed that these vernacular forms controvert the syllabification principles of SA (p. 20), which do not operate nearly so effectively in the vernaculars. Insofar as such a form is incorporated into SA diction, the unacceptable consonant-cluster /ʾsm/ would probably be resolved by the insertion of an indeterminate vowel.

But apart from those cases, Arabic has shown a decided reluctance to using prepositional amplification of a substantive; older writing would normally have paraphrased an expression like 'the man in the moon' by some such wording as 'the man whom we see in the moon'. However, expressions of this kind are beginning to make their way into modern SA, often based on European clichés like 'art for art's sake'.

Adjectival clauses

The amplification of a substantive by means of a sentence structure (the English 'relative clause') provides an example of the survival of a primitive coordination syntax. In ancient Arabic, a clause functioning in this way was structured as an independent sentence embodying a pronoun referring to the amplified entity, and with no other syntactic mark: ⟨a man—I met him yesterday—told me⟩ 'a man whom I met yesterday told me'. This still remains the case in SA when the amplified substantive is undefined, as in the example just quoted.

From the earliest times, however, there existed two sets of entity terms of which the sole function was to be amplified in this way, and which do not convey any other information except of the most minimal kind, namely data relating to gender, number and the person/non-person contrast. One of these sets comprises two items which distinguish between persons (*man*) and non-persons (*mā*), but do not distinguish the gender, number or definitional status of the entity they envisage. Nor is the gender and number of that entity *necessarily* marked even by the pronoun within the clause referring back to those entity terms, for this frequently is a stereotyped masculine singular pronoun, irrespective of the nature of the entity envisaged. A structure *man šāwartu-h^u*, formally analyzable as ⟨person—I have consulted him⟩ may have to be interpreted as 'somebody whom I have consulted' or 'some people whom I have consulted' or 'the person (male or female) whom I have consulted' or 'the people whom I have consulted'.

It is a common stylistic trick to amplify one of these entity terms not only by its own necessary clause structure, but additionally by a prepositional phrase with partitive value, yielding the structure *man šāwartu-hu min$_a$ l'aṭibbā'* ⟨person—I have consulted him—of doctors⟩ 'a/the doctor/doctors whom I have consulted'.

The second set of entity terms of this kind comprises items which distinguish the entity envisaged in respect of gender and number, and have always defined status, but do not distinguish between a personal and a non-personal reference (apart from the fact that the items marked for plurality refer only to persons, cf. p. 39). This set includes a masculine singular *llaḏī*, feminine singular *llatī*, etc. Hence, *llaḏī 'abṣartu-h^u* ⟨that—I have seen him/it⟩ covers 'the (male) person whom I saw' and 'the (masculine) thing which I saw'.

Both sets are thus functionally very similar to demonstratives, from which they differ only in being necessarily followed by an amplifying clause structure.

In SA, it is obligatory to employ an item of the *lladī* set as a functional link between a *defined* substantive and its amplifying clause: contrasting with the undefined structure *'aṭibbā'ᵛ šāwartu-hum* ⟨some doctors—I have consulted them⟩ 'some doctors whom I have consulted', is *l'aṭibbā'ᵛ lladīna šāwartu-hum* ⟨the doctors, those—I have consulted them⟩ 'the doctors whom I have consulted'.[1] The originally demonstrative value of these terms has, however, become much weakened in SA by their automatic employment in those structures, with the result that now, if an explicitly demonstrative sense is intended a demonstrative belonging to the normal sets has to be added: *lladī fa'altu-hᵘ* ⟨the thing—I have done it⟩ 'the thing which I have done' contrasts with *hādā lladī fa'altu-hᵘ* 'this thing which I have done'.[2]

English freely uses a 'relative' clause for either of two distinct logical values. The clause has differentiating value in such a sentence as 'the guest who arrived late missed dinner' which contrasts this guest with other guests who arrived in time; on the other hand, 'the guest, who arrived late, missed dinner' does not imply that there were any other guests at all, but establishes a logical relationship between the two predicates 'arrived late' and 'missed dinner', which in this case is causative ('the guest missed dinner because he arrived late') but could in other contexts be adversative or even simply coordinative. Arabic does sometimes use a clause marked by *lladī* in both these two values, but there is nevertheless a strong tendency to avoid the *lladī* structure when the clause is of the second, non-differentiating type, and to use instead coordination or causative subordination. Anīs Maqdisī writes 'several poets executed a volte-face, like Ruṣāfī, *for he* (*fa-'innahu*, see pp. 64, 97) wrote some odes critical (of his former attitudes)', whereas it would be natural in English to write 'like Ruṣāfī, *who* wrote . . .'

[1] This was not so in archaic Arabic, and the Qur'ān contains instances of defined substantives being followed by a clause structure which later linguistic feeling would have identified as having amplifying function, without the use of this link: e.g. sura 4.171 'Jesus son of Mary is the Apostle of God and is His Word which He cast into Mary', with the simple asyndetic structure *kalimatu-hu 'alqā-hā* ⟨His Word—He cast it⟩, whereas SA would require the contrast between *kalimatᵛ 'alqā-hā* 'a word which he cast' and *kalimatᵛ-hu llatī 'alqā-hā* 'his word which he cast'.

[2] This structure is formally validated by the fact that the initial consonant length of *lladī* is the morpheme of the article, so that the structure embodies the normal requirement (*viz.*, immediately following article) demanded in order that a demonstrative may be followed by an explanatory term (p. 43).

7

SYNTACTIC MARKERS OF NOUNS

The morphology of substantives includes syntactic markers corresponding to the function of the word in the sentence. The full range of these markers (which, however, is partially or wholly neutralized in some instances) distinguishes three kinds of syntactic status:

(i) independent status, belonging to the prime constituents of the sentence, namely the theme, the agent of a verb in a verbal predicate structure, and a noun predicate in a non-verbal predicate structure (see Chapter 9).

(ii) dependent status, belonging to the amplifying term in an annexion structure (p. 45), and to substantives placed after a preposition.

(iii) subordinate status, which belongs to amplifications of the predicate, including the direct object (i.e. an object term not marked by a preposition, see p. 87); and in a few special cases to an amplification of a substantive, e.g. the amplification of decad numerals (p. 61) and limiting amplification of an intensified noun (p. 60).

The markers take the form of variable vowel terminations added after the stem of the word. They are closely associated with another phonetic feature, namely *-n* after a short variable vowel, *-na* or *-ni* after a long variable vowel or *-ay-*. This feature is positionally determined by the following factors: (i) *none* of the items *-n*, *-na*, *-ni* is present in an annexed noun; (ii) the occurrence of *-n* after a short variable vowel is eliminated when the word has the article. These factors account for the alternative possibilities signalized by / in the schematization below.

In order to set out the scheme, nouns must be classified as follows:

(i) those with full range of vowel variation in all circumstances;

(ii) those showing the full range only when they have the article or are annexed, but otherwise show a restricted range of two variations;

(iii) those embodying the external feminine plural morpheme *-āt-*;

(iv) external masculine plurals;

(v) duals;

(vi) those with a word pattern ending in $-R_2iR_3$ where R_3 is *w* or *y*;

(vii) those terminating in *-ā/-an*;

(viii) those terminating in *-ā* without the alternative possibility of *-an*.

In classes (iv) and (v), the morpheme has a double function, marking simultaneously the numerical and the syntactic status. In class (vi), R_3 is eliminated from the word. Classes (ii) and (viii) comprise certain specific word patterns, whether as a whole or to a limited extent when used in certain specific semantic ranges (to take one example, all words used as the personal names of females belong to those classes, though similar word patterns when used otherwise do not necessarily belong to them).

Given this classification we find:

<table>
<tr><th>Class</th><th>Independent</th><th>Dependent</th><th>Subordinate</th></tr>
<tr><td>(i)</td><td>-u/un</td><td>-i/-in</td><td>-a/-an</td></tr>
<tr><td>(ii)</td><td>-u</td><td colspan="2">-a</td></tr>
<tr><td>(iii)</td><td>-u/-un</td><td colspan="2">-i/-in</td></tr>
<tr><td>(iv)</td><td>-ū/-ūn^a</td><td colspan="2">-ī/-īn^a</td></tr>
<tr><td>(v)</td><td>-ā/-ān^i</td><td colspan="2">-ay/-ayn^i</td></tr>
<tr><td>(vi)</td><td colspan="2">$-R_2\bar{\imath}/-R_2in$</td><td>$-R_2iya/R_2iyan$</td></tr>
<tr><td>(vii)</td><td colspan="3">-ā/-an</td></tr>
<tr><td>(viii)</td><td colspan="3">-ā</td></tr>
</table>

Adjectives mirror the substantive which they amplify by showing the same syntactic marker as they would if they stood in the position of the substantive; but since they are divisible into the same classes as detailed above, it can happen that the shape of the morpheme is different as between substantive and adjective, so a substantive of class (i) marked by *-in* may be amplified by an adjective marked by *-a* if the latter belongs to class (ii), and vice versa.

Dual demonstratives show the same syntactic markers as dual substantives; singular and plural demonstratives have no variable syntactic markers. In all cases, however, an accompanying substantive (p. 43) has the marker appropriate to the function of the demonstrative in the sentence, on account of the parity of status between the two terms. The *llaḏī* set of specialized demonstratives (pp. 49–50) similarly show no syntactic variation in singular or plural, but vary in the dual like class (v), in function of their relationship to the main sentence (*not*, as is the case with English 'relative pronouns' like 'whom', 'whose', etc., according to function in the following clause structure); the *man/mā* set has no syntactic markers at all.

The addition of the amplifying pronoun morpheme *-ī* 'my' to a substantive neutralizes its short vowel variations: *baytu-hā*, *bayti-hā*, *bayta-hā* 'her house' are all matched by *bayt-ī* 'my house' irrespective of syntactic position.

The use of this system of marking in its entirety is validated for poetry by the metrical and rhyming systems, and has always been insisted on in the recitation of the Qur'ān. It has equally been a passionately held dogma of the learned classes that it is necessary for 'correct' Arabic (hence the system itself is called *'iʿrāb* 'Arabicization'), and it forms a prime element in the linguistic teaching in schools throughout the Arab world today.

On the other hand, the distinctions had disappeared from the ordinarily spoken language already in or shortly after the eighth century, and this is also the case with the modern vernaculars: the distinctive terminations have been wholly eliminated in classes (i), (ii), (iii) (with the exception of a few words borrowed from the learned language, which retain the *-an* morpheme, as in *'awwalan* 'firstly'), and reduced to non-syntactically-variable number morphemes *-īn* and *-ayn* in classes (iv) and (v). At present, only a small sector of the highest educated Arabic-speaking population is capable of using the system with complete confidence in extempore, unprepared, diction. Some speakers reduce the mental effort needed for operating it by extending the principles of pause (pp. 21–2), which at least eliminate the distinctive short vowel terminations, to the smallest possible speech segments; others, by pronouncing every word as if in pre-pausal position. However, even in such forms of diction, the very close juncture of annexed plus amplifying entity term means that the complete pre-pausal form of the annexed term is not felt possible, and has resulted in retention of the so-called 'feminine' *t* of an annexed word, even though its following vowel may be eliminated: hence the contrasts

with *'iʿrāb*	*li-ddawlati lmiṣriyya*	*li-dawlati miṣr*
without *'iʿrāb*	*li-ddawla lmiṣriyya*	*li-dawlat miṣr*
	'for the Egyptian state'	'for the state of Egypt'

The partial or entire elimination of *'iʿrāb* does not in fact entail significant loss of comprehensibility, since the markers are to a large extent redundant. In an obvious example, since a preposition is always immediately followed by the entity term with which it is syntactically linked, the overt mark of dependent status is in that case superfluous. Even when the substantive with dependent status follows an annexed noun, it would be difficult to find any sentence where elimination of the mark of dependent status would lead to ambiguity; for to treat the two terms as *not* linked by annexion will ordinarily lead to the sentence containing one more entity than can be fitted into any possible structure of it.

The main case in which the system can be said to be functionally significant, and the one to which advocates of the system always appeal, is that of distinguishing the agent (p. 63) from the direct object. Yet even here, the fact that the system itself neutralizes the distinction in a considerable number of cases (nouns ending in *-ā*, substantives with the pronoun *-ī* attached, singular and plural demonstratives, etc.) means that it must often tolerate ambiguities of formal identification of function.[1] Disuse of the system only means extending an area of ambiguity already rooted in the system itself. One is obliged to admit that the system is to a considerable extent an ornament of diction rather than functionally necessary.

There was indeed, in the early decades of this century, a considerable controversy over the 'language problem', in which the extremists on both sides—those who demanded retention of the grammarians' system in its full vigour, and those who advocated a wholesale abandonment of SA in favour of the vernaculars—were opposed by a moderate party, of whom one of the spokesmen was Muḥammad Ḥusayn Haykal, calling for a simplification of SA by omission of *'iʿrāb*. The political trends of Arab nationalism today would make it unthinkable to advocate the fragmentation of the Arabic speaking world by the total abandonment of SA; but little has been heard recently even of the moderates' proposal. I suspect myself that at least one of the reasons for this is the practical difficulty of drafting a code of usage which dispenses with *'iʿrāb*. It would be easy enough to

[1] The system has no means of distinguishing whether *ra'ā 'aḵī mūsā* is intended to signify 'my brother saw Moses' or 'Moses saw my brother'.

lay down that *fī lbayt* should replace *fī lbayti* 'in the house'; but the masculine enclitic pronouns have a vowel quality variation (p. 41) which largely is determined by the *'iʿrāb* of the substantive to which they are attached, and how would one deal with a phrase like *fī bayti-him* 'in their house' (contrasting with *hāḏā baytu-hum* 'this is their house')? To admit into SA **fī bayt-hum* would be a frank surrender to vernacular usage, of which this is characteristic, and is something which it would need a bold innovator to contemplate. This and many other similar problems beset the path of any would-be reformer of SA.

8

ENTITY TERMS: II

Substantive clauses

A proposition which is not the main statement but functions within the main statement as an entity term can (optionally) be marked in English by 'that', as in 'I hope that he's coming today'. The corresponding Arabic functional marker has two morphological shapes, *'an* and *'anna.* Syntactically, these are distinguished by the fact that the former demands that the following clause structure have a verb-predicate at its head, the latter demands a clause structure beginning with an entity term or a preposition.

Semantically, the distinction is slightly more complex. Verbs have two distinctive sets, 'prefix' and 'suffix' (p. 76), so that there are in fact three possibilities: *'an* + prefix set verb, *'an* + suffix set verb, and *'anna* + entity term or prepositional phrase. There is a bipartite functional opposition between the first of these possibilities and the other two (thus cutting across the morphological distinction). The first envisages the proposition embodied in the clause as a mere notion, and represents approximately 'the idea that . . .'; the other two envisage 'the fact that . . .'. The choice between the two structures depends on the context provided by the main proposition into which the clause is fitted. A substantive-clause mentioned as an expectation, possibility, etc., is a notion or idea; the object of knowledge, belief, assertion, etc., is envisaged as a fact. It is, however, not always easy for an English speaker to predict the colouring which an Arabic substantive clause will take in this respect.

Being entity terms, substantive clauses function in the sentence in all the ways that any other entity term does. They can be theme, predicate, object, or placed after a preposition (cf. Biblical English 'after that he had departed', 'for that he was sick'). Theoretically, a substantive clause is always replaceable by a structure centred on a verbal abstract, so that 'that he departed' and 'that he may depart' are replaceable by 'his departure'. In practice, there are idiomatic preferences for one or the other kind of structure, not coincident with English preferences.

A substantive clause can equally function as amplifier of an annexed term, as in 'the absurdity of the-idea-that he may depart'. Here, there is one special case in that an annexed substantive denoting time is commonly followed by a substantive clause without the normal functional marker: so that the clause structure replacing 'the day of his death' exactly reproduces the English structure 'the day he died', and if *'iʿrāb* is used, the word 'day' will have the status of an annexed term in both formulations (verbal abstract structure *yawm*^{v} *mawti-h*^{i}, clause structure *yawm*^{v} *māt*^{a}), and hence is without the article and without terminal *-n* (p. 52).

An alternative to the *'an/'anna* marker is *mā*. In usage, however, the two are not freely interchangeable: 'because of the fact that' can be represented by *li-'anna* or *li-mā*, but 'in spite of the fact that' is *maʿa 'an/maʿa 'anna* and not **maʿa mā*, while 'simultaneously with the fact that' is *ʿinda mā* and never **ʿinda 'an/ʿinda 'anna*.

The intensified noun

A noun pattern *'aR*$_1$*R*$_2$*aR*$_3$ has the semantic value of describing an entity which is intensely, pre-eminently, or even uniquely characterized by some quality. It has commonly been referred to as an adjective,[1] and it does in most instances correspond to a concept expressed in European languages by an adjective; but in the Arabic structures it functions quite as frequently substantivally as adjectivally. It is always in contrast with a noun of some other pattern (from the same root) which does not possess this special intensity: *šāʿir* 'poet' contrasts with *'ašʿar* 'particularly good poet', and *ʿajīb* '(something) marvellous' with *'aʿjab* '(something) particularly marvellous'. But it is not always easy to determine with what pattern the intensified noun contrasts: *'aḥkam* serves as the intensified contrast both to *ḥakīm* 'wise (man)' and to *muḥkam* 'firm/solid'.

Morphologically, one must distinguish two varieties of these nouns. When not carrying the article, *'aR*$_1$*R*$_2$*aR*$_3$ is a stable pattern not admitting any morphological indications of gender and number. With the article, *l'aR*$_1$*R*$_2$*aR*$_3$ is the masculine singular item in a set which comprises also feminine singular *lR*$_1$*uR*$_2$*R*$_3$*ā*, masculine plural *l'aR*$_1$*āR*$_2$*iR*$_3$, feminine plural *lR*$_1$*uR*$_2$*aR*$_3$; also duals of the normal types and, in a few cases, masculine and feminine plural with external marker (p. 39). While the differentiation between the stable and the

[1] For simplicity, I have so referred to it in *Written Arabic*, ch. 10.

gender-and-number-differentiated varieties can be overall presented as conditioned by the absence or presence of the article, this is not the whole of the story; some exceptions do occur (see below).

Probably the commonest structural occurrence of the intensified pattern is its use as an annexed substantive. When it is annexed to an undefined substantive, the annexion is a relationship of identity or explanation: *'aʿjab*^{v} *manẓar* is analyzable as ⟨the pre-eminently marvellous thing which can be called 'a sight'⟩. It will be observed that this structure generates a conflict between the formal and the logical status of the phrase in respect of definition; such phrases are formally and grammatically undefined, yet the concept of distinctiveness (and hence lack of ambiguity) implied by the pattern itself gives the phrase a degree of logical definition, and this structure is the normal equivalent of the English superlative, 'the most marvellous sight'.

When it is annexed to a defined entity term, the English equivalent is also a 'superlative', but in this case the annexion relationship is partitive, and the sense of the phrase differs according to whether the amplifying term is singular or plural. A plural denotes a category within which the entity described by the intensified pattern constitutes one item: *'aʿjab*^{v} *lmanāẓir* 'the most marvellous of sights'.[1] But a defined singular, in order to preserve the partitive relationship, must be envisaged as fragmented in some way, e.g. *'aʿjab*^{v} *lmanẓar* 'the most marvellous feature of the sight'.

Among the values of the preposition *min* is 'in comparison with', exemplified in the idiomatic phrase *'ayna hāḏā min ḏālik*^{a} ⟨where is this in comparison with that?⟩ 'this bears no comparison with that'. *min* used in conjunction with an intensified noun therefore gives the latter the value of an English 'comparative': *'aʿjab*^{v} *min hāḏā* ⟨something pre-eminently marvellous in comparison with this⟩ 'something more marvellous than this'. This structure is almost always undefined: for the concept 'the more marvellous thing than this' is not one that normally demands expression, and is indeed not easily envisageable. In the rare instances where it is called for, the lack of gender and number differentiation characteristic of the undefined form, which is so much more common, is carried over into the defined form: *ṭā'irat*^{v} *'asraʿ*^{v} *min*$_{a}$ *ṣṣawt* 'an aircraft swifter than sound' has generated *ṭṭā'irat*^{v} *l'asraʿ*^{v} *min*$_{a}$ *ṣṣawt* 'the supersonic aircraft'.

The intensified pattern, particularly when it functions as a predicate, can be used in isolation so long as an appropriate amplification can be understood from the context, and it is then the context which will

[1] A defined dual is analysable in the same terms as a plural, i.e. 'the . . . er one of the two . . .'. But if an intensified pattern is annexed to an undefined dual, the sense is 'the . . . est pair of . . .', e.g. *'ašhar*^{v} *muḥibbayn* 'the most famous pair of lovers'.

determine the differentiation between 'comparative' and 'superlative' usage: 'there are many ways of doing this, but my way is easiest', and 'there is another way of doing this, but my way is easier' can both be presented as *sabīl-ī 'aysar*^{u}, understanding in the former instance *'aysaru kulli-hā* 'the easiest of all of them' and in the latter *'aysaru min ḏālika ssabīl* 'easier than that way'.

English 'superlatives' embrace two kinds of superlative concept. There is a limited superiority in respect of which the entity so qualified transcends only a limited group of entities within its own category, as in 'the greatest sin I have ever committed', which allows the possibility that other people may have committed even greater sins. On the other hand, there is absolute superiority when 'the greatest sin' implies 'the greatest of all sins whatsoever'.

Limited superiority is expressed in Arabic only by structures in which the intensified pattern functions as annexed substantive. The defined intensified pattern when functioning as an adjective connotes only the absolute type of superiority, not the limited type described first. Absolute superiority is often associated with cliché expressions which have to all intents the unique value of a substantive of single application marked in English by the use of capitals: *lḥarb*^{v} *l'uẓmā* is 'the Great War', not 'the greatest war (within some special group of wars)' which is *'a'ẓam*^{v} *ḥarb*^{in} or *'a'ẓam*^{v} *lḥurūb*^{i}; *lmasjid*^{v} *l'aqṣā*[1] is 'the Far Mosque', a designation applied only to the mosque adjacent to the Dome of the Rock in Jerusalem, not to e.g. 'the farthest mosque from the city centre'; *dduwal*^{v} *lkubrā* is 'the Great Powers'.

In other cases absolute superiority may be marked in English by the use of a different word: *l'a'lā*[1] functioning as an adjective does not cover the whole field of 'highest' (for that includes cases where the entity is only highest within a limited group), but is better rendered by 'supreme', as in *lmaḥkamat*^{v} *l'ulyā* 'the Supreme Court', and *lmaṯal*^{v} *l'a'lā* ⟨the highest pattern of all⟩ 'the Ideal'.

Expressions of this kind do, however, generate secondary uses beside this one of absolute superiority; and such usages carry the gender differentiation of the intensified pattern into the undefined form: *maḥkamat*^{v} *'ulyā* 'a supreme court', *muṯul*^{v} *'ulyā* 'some ideals'. Note also *lmaḥkamat*^{v} *l'ulyā fī wāšinṭūn* 'the supreme court in Washington' implying 'the highest of all courts namely the one in Washington', which contrasts with the limited superiority implied if the phrase were taken to mean 'the highest of several courts which are in Washington' (Arabic *'a'lā lmaḥākimi fī w.*)

There are a few anomalies. The nouns *ḵayr* 'good', *šarr* 'bad', *'āḵir* 'last', *'awwal* 'first', which are not intensified patterns (though 'first'

[1] *'aqṣā* and *'a'lā* are both *'af'al* patterns from roots with R_3 a semivowel, represented by the vowel length of the *ā* (p. 32).

may perhaps be derived morphologically from an original intensified pattern *'*a'wal*), are nevertheless often incorporated in structures similar to those of the intensified pattern and having the same values: hence, *k̲ayr*^{v} *l'umūr*^{i} 'the best thing', *sabīl*^{v} *k̲ayr*^{v} *min hād̲ā* 'a better way than this', *'awwal*^{v} *'amr*^{in} 'the first thing', *'awwal*^{v} *l'amr*^{i} 'the first part of the thing'.

The concept 'middle' is one that does not normally admit of degrees of comparison, and consequently the simple pattern *wasīṭ* and the intensified pattern *'awsaṭ* are synonymous; in practice there is some preference for the latter, and indeed the latter is almost exclusively used in the substantival function, as in *'awsaṭ*^{v} *'awlād-ī* ⟨the middle one of my sons⟩ 'my middle son', *'awsaṭ*^{v} *ššahr*^{i} 'the middle part of the month'. In the adjectival function one encounters *lqurūn*^{v} *lwusṭā* 'the Middle Ages', *nuqṭat*^{v} *wusṭā* 'a mid point'; but also *lmu'jam*^{v} *lwasīṭ* 'the Intermediate Dictionary'.

The fact that annexion of an intensified pattern is always partitive or identificatory in nature means that limiting annexion (p. 47) cannot be used; in lieu, the limiting term is marked by the morpheme of subordinate status. Contrasting with the non-intensified structure *'ajīb*^{v} *ssam'i* ⟨marvellous in respect of hearing⟩ 'marvellous to hear', one has *'a'jab*^{v}*-hum sam'an* 'the most marvellous of them to hear' and *'a'jab*^{v} *min-hu sam'an* 'more marvellous to hear than him'. This structure has a special usefulness in resolving ambiguities over the contrasting non-intensified pattern: in the example quoted earlier, the ambiguity of *'aḥkam* could be avoided by adding the limiting term *ḥikmatan* 'in respect of wisdom' or *'iḥkāman* 'in respect of solidity', either as amplification of *'aḥkam* itself or of some more colourless and generalized intensified pattern; a particularly common generalized term in such structures is *'ašadd* 'more/most/very extreme', e.g. *'ašadd*^{v} *rag̲batan* ⟨more/most/very extreme in respect of desire⟩ 'more/most/very desirous'. Quite apart from cases of actual ambiguity, this structure is far more favoured than a European would anticipate.

Designations of colour, etc.

Terms denoting colour and undesirable physical characteristics ('crooked', 'lame', etc.) were almost certainly in origin intensified patterns of the same type as already described. In the historical language, however, they have evolved into an independent word class distinguished by their own characteristic differentiation in the number and gender patterns, which in these words are:

masculine singular $'aR_1R_2aR_3$
feminine singular $R_1aR_2R_3\bar{a}'$
common gender plural $R_1uR_2R_3$

It will be seen that these differences from the ordinary intensified pattern are only very minor, and there is every likelihood that they were originally only dialectal variations, subsequently erected into functionally differentiating criteria.

A feature shared by all words of the pattern *'a*R_1R_2*a*R_3, both those functioning as intensified terms and colour words, is that their *'iʿrāb* is of classes (ii) and (viii) (p. 52); they therefore never have the terminal *-n*, and (when not annexed and not carrying the article) they admit only two distinctive syntactic markers.

Numerals

The numeral system of SA is complicated, and nowhere more so than in the 11–19 range. I shall not therefore attempt here a full analysis of the latter.

When used for the simple enumeration of a group of undefined entities, the SA numerals are substantives to which the numbered entity functions as amplifier. The numerals 3–10 are *annexed* to a plural, those for 100 upwards to a singular: *'ašr*^{v} *sā'āt*^{in} ⟨une dizaine d'heures⟩ 'ten hours', *mi'at*^{v} *sāʿa*^{tin} ⟨une centaine d'heure⟩ 'a hundred hours'. Decad numerals and 11–19 are not annexed, but amplified by a singular substantive marked for subordinate status, *sitt*$^{\bar{u}/\bar{\imath}}$*na sāʿa*^{tan} ⟨sixty in respect of hour⟩ 'sixty hours'.

The substantive numerals 3–10 have the odd feature that they exhibit the 'feminine' marker when the numbered entity is masculine in the singular, and are not so marked when it is feminine: *ṯalāṯ*^{v} *sāʿāt*^{in} 'three hours', *ṯalāṯat*^{v} *'aʿwām*^{in} 'three years' (singular *ʿām* being masculine).

There are two distinctive patterns associated with the 3–10 range, of which $R_1\bar{a}R_2iR_3$ marks place in a series (this pattern applicable also to the concept 'second' in a series), and $R_1uR_2R_3$ a fraction: *lbāb*^{v} *ṯṯāliṯ* 'the third chapter', *ṯulṯ*^{v} *mīl*^{in} 'one third of a mile'. From 20 upwards, the numerals marking place in a series are not morphologically distinguished from the enumerative ones: *ṯalāṯ*$^{\bar{u}/\bar{\imath}}$*na bāb*^{an} 'thirty chapters', *lbāb*^{v} *ṯṯalāṯ*$^{\bar{u}/\bar{\imath}}$*n*^{a} 'the thirtieth chapter'.

In enumeration of defined entities, ancient usage, which is still current in the 3–10 range, prescribed that enumerator and enumerated entity should be in appositional relationship, with full parity of status; this implies that both have identical marking for syntactic status, that both must be marked for definition by the article, and that their relative order is indifferent. Hence, *lqaṣā'id*^{v} *ssabʿ*^{v} or *ssabʿ*^{v} *lqaṣā'id*^{v} 'the seven odes'. From 20 upwards, however, there has been since medieval times a strong tendency towards modelling the defined structure on the undefined one and placing the numeral first, simply with the article attached to the numeral. This creates no formal problems in the decad numerals, where *l'arba*$^{\text{ʿū/ī}}$*na liṣṣan* ⟨the forty in respect of thief⟩ 'the forty thieves' does not offend against any general principle. But beyond the decads, syntactic difficulties are encountered in conflating the structure *mi'at*^{v} *mankūb*^{in} 'a hundred victims' with *mankūb*$^{\text{ū/ī}}$ *lfayaḍān* 'the flood victims' to produce 'the hundred flood victims'; yet it would be normal in SA to write *lmi'at*^{v} *mankūbi lfayaḍān*, in defiance of the solecism (traditionally speaking) of attaching the article to the annexed numeral.[1]

In compound numerals, SA generally follows the same principle as German, placing the highest digit first except that the unit digit precedes the tens digit: ⟨one thousand and three hundred and five and forty⟩ '1345'.

[1] This resembles in essence that other modernism described on p. 48, where the article is prefixed to an annexion structure instead of being infixed.

9

THEME AND PREDICATE

Theme

Normally, the theme occupies first position in the sentence, if one excludes functionals from consideration. The term functioning as theme may be *any* entity involved in the statement, and will (subject to certain specific exceptional cases) be reflected in a pronoun later in the sentence, referring back to it. Structures which in English are purely colloquial such as 'This guy, he ups and hits me' and 'This guy, I ups and hits him', are the norm in Arabic.

Formal structural analysis, however, does not always yield the same result as a logical analysis. Some manifestations of this will be discussed below; but of major general importance is the contrast between a thematic sentence structure, in which the theme occupies the first position, and a verbal sentence structure in which a verb predicate comes first. As an alternative to the thematic structure ⟨the king, he died⟩ there is the verbal structure ⟨died the king⟩. Clearly, any difference there may be between these two structures lies solely in the speaker's mind; the historical fact which he is stating is identical in both cases. 'The king' has therefore the same logical function in the two sentence forms, in spite of the structural difference; this *may* reflect some difference in the speaker's mental attitude to the fact he is stating, though in some cases this is not so, the choice of structure being determined by grammatical considerations (as e.g. in the structures following *'an/'anna*, see p. 56). But the existence of the structural differentiation does demand the employment of a special terminology for an entity which is logically the theme, but is embodied in a verbal sentence structure like ⟨died the king⟩: I use 'agent' for the logical theme placed after its verb predicate, when such a distinction is needed.

In principle, a theme shows the syntactic marker of independent status, in so far as it is morphologically capable of being distinctively marked. But there are some functionals which impart to the theme the status of a direct object; and the theme is then marked as if it had subordinate status (this includes the choice of an enclitic pronoun item instead of an independent one). Probably, such functionals had originally some degree of verbal force, and this is best illustrated by the functional *'inna*: one can conjecture that this may originally have signified something like 'behold'; and the English Biblical structure 'consider the lilies of the field, they toil not' has precisely the structure of an Arabic thematic sentence with *'inna* prefixed. So far as medieval and SA are concerned, such a value has either been completely lost—so that the above-mentioned sentence has purely and simply the value of modern English 'the lilies of the field do not toil'—or has merged into some other semantic value; after the coordinating functional *fa* (p. 97) for instance, *'inna* often reinforces the causal value of that functional. Other functionals which impart object status to the theme include *'anna* 'that' (p. 56) and *la'alla* 'perhaps'.

So far, we have seen three ways of beginning a sentence, (i) with a theme having independent status, (ii) with a verb predicate, (iii) with an 'objectivizing' functional plus theme marked as for subordinate status. Yet it is very common for a sentence to begin with a prepositional phrase or other adverbial (see p. 88), as in 'on the following day, the king died' or simply 'the following day, the king died'. There is little doubt that, logically, the initial phrase is here too a theme, having as its predicate an encapsulated sentence structure of verb + agent, or secondary theme + predicate (pp. 66, 70).

There are several reasons why the grammarians have been reluctant to admit such a phrase as having the formal status of a theme. The main ones are that the phrase is marked as having subordinate status *without* the presence of an objectivizing functional; and that the encapsulated structure contains no pronoun referring back to the preceding entity term. There is a contrast between the formal thematic structure *lyawmu ttālī māta fī-hi lmalik* ⟨the following day died on it the king⟩, with *lyawmu* 'the day' marked by the morpheme of independent status, and the encapsulated structure containing the referential phrase *fī-hi* 'on it', and the *not* formally thematic structure *lyawma ttaliya māta lmalik*, with *lyawma* marked as having subordinate status and no referential pronoun. The latter structure, ⟨the following day, died the king⟩, is formally a verbal sentence structure with the adverbial amplification of the predicate placed in front of the verb predicate itself. Yet there are some clear indications that an initial phrase of this kind is indeed logically a theme.

It is a cardinal principle that a theme must be at least logically defined, for the information conveyed by the predicate is useless to the hearer unless he can with certainty identify the topic about which it is stated: 'this man is fallible' and 'man is fallible' are both statements about a defined entity (generically defined in the second case because applicable to the whole category of men), but 'some man or other is fallible' conveys no useful information to the hearer. Exceptions are apparent and not real: 'every man' and 'no man', though expressed by formally undefined terms, are logically defined because admitting no uncertainty of identification (p. 37). Further, any sort of amplification of a substantive is regarded as sufficiently narrowing the area of uncertainty to permit it functioning as theme even if formally undefined. And the objectivizing functionals, presumably because of their original verbal force, also allow an undefined theme following. But the principle holds full force in the case of an adverbial phrase functioning informally as theme, which must embody a defined entity term, apart from a few clichés: it is permissible to write 'one day, the king went out hunting', this being a cliché way of beginning a narrative, but it is not permissible to write *'with a gun, the king went out hunting'.

The requirement for a defined term as logical theme is also apparent even in a verbally structured sentence. A communication consisting only of verb plus undefined agent, such as 'some king or other died', is valueless to the hearer and non-viable,[1] just as much when verbally structured as it would have been if 'king' had been improperly placed as a formal theme. But ⟨died in that year a king⟩ is viable because the defined adverbial functions as logical theme. In one sense, therefore, an agent term can be a member of the logical predicate as much as an object term is.

Occasionally, the logically thematic status of an adverbial is demonstrated by the absence of any formal theme. 'He told me that in the coastal regions thereof they catch fish' requires a thematic structure after the functional 'that' (p. 56), and a formal thematic structuring would thus require the extrapolation of 'they' as theme, *'ak̲bara-nī 'anna-hum fī sawāḥili-hā yaṣīdūna l'asmāk*. Yet instances can be found in which this is not done, and the sentence is structured as *'ak̲bara-nī 'anna fī sawāḥili-hā yaṣīdūna l'asmāk* where it is clear that *fī sawāḥili-hā* 'in the coastal regions thereof' is functioning as quasi-theme.

Moreover, there is a functional *'ammā* which can be placed before the theme, in order to mark it as emphatically contrasted with some other entity. English normally marks this kind of emphasis only by tonal variation, as in the simple statement:

my mother is Scots *versus* my father is Irish; my mother is Scots

[1] This remark does not exclude the viability of such a structure in cases where the formal agent is a logical predicate (i.e. where the intention is 'the person who has died was a king').

In SA, it is obligatory, when this functional has been used, to mark the peginning of the predicate by *fa*. Whatever precedes *fa* must therefore be reckoned as theme, and it is quite common to find an adverbial in this position, functioning as logical theme: *hāḏā mā jarā fī miṣra 'ammā fī ššaʼmi fa-ḵtalafat 'aḥwālu lbilādi ʽan ḏālik*[a] 'this is what happened in Egypt; in Syria [with raised tone], the conditions of the country were different from that'. The use of *fa* to mark the beginning of the predicate is also, in SA, common after an adverbial logical theme even when not marked by *'ammā*: *wa-maʽa ḏālika fa-ljawābu sahl* 'nevertheless, the answer is easy'.

Predicate

A predicate may be:

(i) classificatory, assigning the theme to membership of a category, as in 'Joe is rich' and 'Joe is a rich man', both assigning him to the category of rich people.

(ii) identificatory, where theme and predicate are two known and recognizable entities which are stated to be one and the same, as in 'Joe is the founder of the tennis club'.

(iii) locatory, indicating the theme's position, as in 'the meeting is on Friday', 'the meeting is in the village hall', 'the meeting is under Joe's chairmanship', 'the fact is beyond dispute'.

(iv) a statement of an event in which the theme (or agent) plays a part, as in 'Joe opened the meeting'.

Identificatory predicates are by their nature independent of a time factor, that is, an indication of the temporal relationship between the moment of utterance and the situation pictured by the predicate. Once both 'Joe' and 'the founder of the tennis club' have become recognizable entities, a correctly made identification of the two will be as valid next week as it is today or was yesterday. Events on the other hand are necessarily time-sited, even if the siting remains only vaguely stated or wholly unmentioned. The other two kinds of predicate are ambivalent and capable of being either timeless like the identificatory predicate ('the horse is a quadruped', 'Colombo is near the Equator'), or temporally sited like the event predicate ('Joe is rich', 'Joe is in his back garden').

In English, all predicates are marked as such by a verb, and English verbs incorporate time contrasts which are thereby introduced into predicates even where time is intrinsically irrelevant: the 'is' of 'Joe is in his back garden' contrasts validly with the 'was' of 'Joe was in his back garden', whereas the 'is' of 'the horse is a quadruped' conveys no meaningful distinction of this kind. This is not so in Arabic: predicates may be expressed either by a verb or by a non-verbal structure; non-verbal predicates are in themselves not time-marked at all, and any time relevance they may have is derivable only from the context in which they are placed, or by the addition of a time-marking adverbial; and even the verb has considerably less time significance than the English verb.

The non-verbal predicate is a noun or prepositional phrase, marked as having predicative function by structural means only. For the morpheme of independent status is not distinctive of a predicate, being shared also by the theme (p. 64); and both prepositional phrases and some types of noun (pp. 52, vii, viii) are incapable of such marking in any case. The noun or prepositional phrase predicate can be called 'simple' in contrast to the complex predicate, i.e. a clause structure which in itself could be a viable independent sentence.

A noun functioning as simple non-verbal predicate with classificatory value is recognizable as such by a contrast between definition of the theme (p. 65) and indefinition of the predicate term: given a sequence of defined term followed by undefined term, the latter is a predicate. Consequently, if the defined term *šakwā-hu* 'his complaint' is followed by the undefined *murra*, the latter is a predicate translating the English 'is bitter'; but if the second term matches the first in definitional status then its function is that of amplification, as in *šakwā-hu lmurra* 'his bitter complaint' and *šakwā murra* 'a bitter complaint'.

In so far as the predicate term in this structure is a noun capable of functioning both substantivally and adjectivally, predicative function neutralizes the substantive/adjective distinction, and it would be impossible to say whether *ʿādil*, functioning as predicate, represents 'is just' or 'is a just man'; nor does the fact that such a noun is marked for gender and number correspondingly to the gender and number status of the theme really provide any evidence, for *lmalikatu ʿādila* could be envisaged as 'the queen is just' or as 'the queen is a just woman'. Predicate substantives not capable of functioning as adjectives have their own inherent status in this respect and cannot adapt in this way: *l'asārā ṣuʿūba* 'the prisoners are a difficulty'. But a generalized pronoun or demonstrative (pp. 41–2) theme adopts gender and number marking corresponding to a substantive predicate (whether the latter be classificatory or identificatory): *hiya ṣuʿūba* 'it is a difficulty', *hāḏihi ṣuʿūba* 'this is a difficulty' and *hāḏihi ṣuʿūbat-ī* 'this is my difficulty' all show feminine marking of the theme corresponding to the feminine grammatical status of the predicate term *ṣuʿūba*.

In situations where the theme is a pronoun (such being incapable of amplification, pp. 42–3), a defined term which follows it is necessarily an identificatory predicate. Given the theme 'he/it(masc.)' expressed either by the independent form *huwa* or by the enclitic item *-hu* after an objectivizing functional (p. 64), the placing after it of a defined term such as 'the founder of the club' confers on the latter the status of predicate so that it translates 'is the founder of the club'. The same is true of a demonstrative theme, provided that the definition of the phrase following it is effected otherwise than by the article at the head of the phrase: *hāḏā mu'assisu nnādī* 'this is the founder of the club' contrasts with *hāḏā lmu'assis* 'this founder', and also with *mu'assisu nnādī hāḏā* 'this founder of the club' (p. 43).

Similar structures, where a defined term functions as an identificatory predicate, are found when there is no possibility of misinterpreting the following defined term as an amplification of the preceding one: *ḥukmu lqāḍī 'iʿdāmu rrajul* 'the judge's verdict is the man's execution', since the verbal abstract *'iʿdām* 'execution' cannot function as an adjective but is necessarily a substantive. Where this is not so, the simple predicate must (and *can* otherwise) be replaced by a complex clause predicate with pronoun as secondary theme: *hāḏā huwa lmu'assis* ⟨this man, he is the founder⟩ 'this is the founder'.

The marker of a locatory predicate is a zero syntagmeme: namely, the *absence* of any item in the sentence which might indicate that the locatory phrase is *not* a predicate. If a theme 'the meeting' is followed by the locatory phrase 'on Friday the 13th' and nothing else, the locatory phrase must be a predicate translating 'is on Friday the 13th'. If the sentence contains something else which is a viable predicate, then the locatory phrase is a prepositional amplification of the theme, as in 'the meeting on Friday the 13th is a bad omen'. Ambiguity is created if the further phrase is itself locatory, and it may well be formally impossible to tell which of the two locatory phrases is the predicate, i.e. to distinguish between 'the meeting is on Friday after lunch' and 'the meeting on Friday is after lunch'.

One particularly common simple predicate structure which needs special attention is the case of a prepositional phrase incorporating a defined entity term and functioning as theme (p. 64), followed by an undefined substantive functioning as predicate: *fī hāḏā lmawḍiʿi qaṣr* 'in this place is a castle'. My analysis here runs counter to that of the Arab grammarians, who identify the prepositional phrase as predicate and the substantive as theme, and are hence obliged to say that a theme *can* be undefined *if* it follows a prepositional predicate. I do not myself believe this to be the case: 'castle' in such a statement is clearly a classificatory predicate whose communication value resides in stating what sort of a thing 'this place' contains, and English shows an instinctive appreciation of the predicative function of 'castle' by the alternative structure 'there is a castle in this place' which sets 'castle' in the normal predicative position after 'is'. The sole reason for

TYPES OF PREDICATE

(0 indicates that the sequence is not a predicate structure)

<table>
<tr><th colspan="2" rowspan="3">Second →
First sentence member ↓</th><th colspan="3">Entity term</th><th rowspan="3">Locatory phrase</th><th rowspan="3">Verb with differentiation of number</th></tr>
<tr><th rowspan="2">Defined</th><th colspan="2">Undefined</th></tr>
<tr><th>Not participle</th><th>Participle</th></tr>
<tr><td rowspan="3">Defined entity term</td><td>Independent pronoun</td><td rowspan="2">Identificatory</td><td rowspan="3">Classificatory</td><td rowspan="3">Classificatory
or
Future event</td><td rowspan="3">Locatory</td><td rowspan="3">Event
or
Classificatory</td></tr>
<tr><td>Demonstrative not followed immediately by article</td></tr>
<tr><td>Other types</td><td rowspan="2">0</td></tr>
<tr><td colspan="2">Locatory phrase including defined entity term</td><td colspan="2">‘There is a . . .’</td><td colspan="2">0</td></tr>
<tr><td colspan="2">Verb without differentiation of number</td><td colspan="3">Event or classificatory</td><td colspan="2">0</td></tr>
</table>

the grammarians' analysis lies in the fact that if an 'objectivizing' functional is placed before such a structure the marker of subordinate status is borne by the undefined term instead of the defined (logical) theme, so that one finds *samiʿtu ʾanna fī hāḏā lmawḍiʿi qaṣran* 'I have heard that there is a castle in this place'.

A clause predicate may consist of a secondary theme plus simple predicate. The latter may be classificatory, ⟨Joe, his brother is rich⟩; or identificatory, ⟨Joe, his brother is the founder of the club⟩; or locatory, ⟨Joe, his brother is in America⟩.

Alternatively, the clause predicate may have a structure consisting of verb plus agent, the agent being either a pronoun referring back to the theme as in ⟨Joe, he has died⟩, or some other entity as in ⟨Joe, has died his brother⟩ 'Joe's brother has died'.

The nature of the Arabic verb predicate is more fully discussed in the following chapters, but it is appropriate to call attention here to an anomalous type of predicate structure which embodies a participle as simple predicate. This structure is formally identical with a classificatory or identificatory statement, but is commonly used for the statement of a future event: *ʾana muk̲biru-k*^{a}, which on general principles would have been expected to mean 'I am your informant', is employed to state the future event 'I will inform you' (see further p. 79).

10

THE VERB

The Arabic verb is an amalgam of two semantic elements, a pronoun theme and a predicate. A verb can in consequence function if need be as a complete sentence: *mātat* 'she died'. Each of its two elements has a morphological expression differing from that of the corresponding element in a non-verbal predicate structure. The predicate element in a verb is *either* event-stating *or* classificatory. In ancient Arabic there were some verbs which conveyed a locatory predicate, but this phenomenon no longer appears in SA, though it forms the basis on which several of the modifying verbs (p. 80) have evolved.

A verb stating a classificatory predicate differs little in sense from a structure consisting of independent or 'objectivized' pronoun plus simple predicate; the difference cannot be reflected in English. 'It is difficult' corresponds both to *huwa ṣaʿb* (independent pronoun followed by simple noun predicate) and to *yaṣʿub* in which /*y*/ represents the pronoun theme 'it' and the rest of the word the predicative element 'is difficult'. The difference between the two structures lies solely in the fact that the verb has two parallel sets with semantic contrasts; hence *yaṣʿub* implies certain contrasts with the parallel item in the other set, which is not the case with *huwa ṣaʿb* which does nothing more than to assign the theme to the category of 'difficult things'.

The pronoun element in a verb faithfully reflects the gender and number of the preceding entity term to which it refers, whether that entity be something mentioned in a previous sentence, or a theme to which the verb functions as clause predicate. The pronoun elements /*-at*/ alluding to a feminine singular, and /*-na*/ alluding to a plurality of females, are amalgamated with the predicate element /*jalas*/ to produce *’uḵt-ī jalasat* ⟨my sister, she sat⟩ and *’aḵawāt-ī jalasna* ⟨my sisters, they sat⟩.

But if the verb is followed by a substantive or demonstrative agent, the element in it other than the predicate reflects at most the gender of the agent, and is morphologically congruous with a singular pronoun element; while occasionally even the masculine versus feminine contrast is not marked, so that the congruity is with a masculine singular pronoun element, wholly irrespective of the nature of the following agent. It is hence very doubtful whether it is proper to call the extra-predicative element in such a verb a ‘pronoun’ at all: even in so far as it is marked as feminine it merely signals an expectation of a feminine agent of some kind to follow. Thus the two possible thematic structures representing ‘my sisters sat on this sofa’ have differing verbs according to which entity term is extrapolated as theme: ⟨my sisters, they sat (*jalasna*) on this sofa⟩ but ⟨this sofa, sat (*jalasat*) my sisters on it⟩.

Verb stems

Before examining the verb in detail, it must be said that the verb containing three root consonants (p. 32) is only a primary type or ‘stem’, and that there are usually a varying number of secondary stems in which the root consonants are accompanied by additional phonetic elements.

In SA, the repertory of commonly used secondary stems runs to nine items, but no one root generates all the theoretically possible stems; the average range is about four or five stems.

Each stem has an independent lexical value for its predicate element, and from this point of view is an independent verb; stem analysis merely furnishes a convenient classification of the morphological features of a given verb.

The pronoun element, which appears in two forms, one suffixed and one prefixed, is morphologically identical in all verb stems. The predicate element shows a morphological pattern characteristic both of the particular stem, and of the verb set (prefix-pronoun or suffix-pronoun) within that stem: basically, consonants mark the stem, while the vowel pattern distinguishes the prefix set from the suffix set. In making this formulation, however, one must stipulate that the phonological element of vowel length has, in two of the secondary stems, to be reckoned as a consonant.

In the primary stem, the structure of the predicate element is $R_1aR_2vR_3$/ for the suffix set and /$aR_1R_2vR_3$/ for the prefix set, v being a vowel whose quality is lexically determined in the case of each individual verb. In secondary stems, the vowel pattern is uniform for all verbs assignable to a given stem.

The secondary stems group as follows:

(i) three characterized by one consonant additional to the root consonants;
(ii) one by two additional consonants;
(iii) three by the phonological item of length;
(iv) two by the item of length plus a further consonant.

	Suffix set pattern	Prefix set pattern
Group (i)	$'aR_1R_2aR_3/$	$/uR_1R_2iR_3/$
	$nR_1aR_2aR_3/$	$/anR_1aR_2iR_3/$
	$R_1taR_2aR_3/$[1]	$/aR_1taR_2iR_3/$[1]
Group (ii)	$staR_1R_2aR_3/$	$/astaR_1R_2iR_3/$
Group (iii)	$R_1\bar{a}R_2aR_3/$	$/uR_1\bar{a}R_2iR_3/$
	$R_1a\overline{R_2}aR_3/$	$/uR_1a\overline{R_2}iR_3/$
	$R_1R_2a\overline{R_3}/$	$/aR_1R_2a\overline{R_3}/$
Group (iv)	$taR_1\bar{a}R_2aR_3/$	$/ataR_1\bar{a}R_2aR_3/$
	$taR_1a\overline{R_2}aR_3/$	$/ataR_1a\overline{R_2}aR_3/$

It will be observed that a peculiarity of the first-mentioned stem in Group (i) is that the characteristic stem consonant ' is not present in the prefix set: this is distinguished from the prefix set of the primary stem only by the vowel pattern.

Roots of four consonants $R_1R_2R_3R_4$ are fitted into this system by treating their $R_2R_3R_4$ as if they were $\overline{R_2}R_3$ and employing the vowel patterns appropriate to one of the two stems characterized by $\overline{R_2}$.

Each stem has its own matching verbal abstract and participles. Here too, the characteristic ' is not present in the participles; they are however very clearly distinguished from those of the primary stem, being $muR_1R_2iR_3$ and $muR_1R_2aR_3$ for that stem against the primary stem ones $R_1\bar{a}R_2iR_3$ and $maR_1R_2\bar{u}R_3$.

Usually, all verbs sharing the same root have some slight degree of semantic relationship with each other, but the lexical values of the occurring stems show enormous variety. Attempts to define the shade of meaning associated with a particular stem as such can only be very imprecise, and it is impossible to deduce the lexical meaning of a verb simply by considering its stem and the 'basic' root concept. Such a procedure takes one usually no further than does a consideration of

[1] When R_1 is one of the four velarized alveolars (p. 18), the extension of the velarization prosody to the characteristic stem consonant, with which it is in immediate contact, is marked in the script: hence *ṣṭadam*/(root *ṣdm*),/*aṭṭaliʿ*/ (root *ṭlʿ*), etc.

the original meaning of a Latin verb towards an understanding of the lexical value of a modern English verb derived from the Latin: one can easily understand how the modern meaning of 'I respected him' has evolved from the Latin *respexi eum* 'I looked attentively at him', but one could not achieve an appreciation of the sense of the English verb merely by stating the sense of the Latin verb from which it is derived. But bearing this caution in mind, it is possible to quote some fairly characteristic lexical values associated with the secondary stems.

'*RRR* is often factitive as in '*aḵbara-hā* 'he informed her' versus *ḵabarat-hu* 'she was aware of it'; or ergative as in '*ajlasa-nī* 'he sat me down'; but there is a very large range of verbs having neither of these implications, often being intransitive—'*abṣara-hᵘ* 'he perceived it', '*adbarᵃ* 'he turned back', '*aqbalᵃ* 'he moved forward', '*aflasᵃ* 'he went bankrupt', '*aḥabba-hā* 'he loved her', '*aḥāṭū bi-nā* 'they surrounded us', '*aqfarat₁ lbilād* 'the country went to waste'.

nRRR is in the majority of cases the intransitive counterpart of a transitive primary stem—*nkasarᵃ* 'it broke' versus *kasara-hᵘ* 'he broke it', *nqaṭaʿa lḥablᵘ* 'the rope parted' versus *qaṭaʿa lḥablᵃ* 'he severed the rope', *nṣarafat* 'she turned away' versus *ṣaraftu-hā* 'I turned her away'.

RtRR, in so far as one can make any generalization about it, is associated with an interiorization of experience which is alien to English linguistic feeling but often underlies French 'reflexive' verbs —*btadarat* 'she hastened (elle s'est dépêchée)', *štakaytu-hᵘ* 'I complained of it (je m'en suis plaint)', *ftaḵarat* 'she boasted (elle s'est vantée)'; other examples are *stamaʿa 'ilay-hī* 'he listened to it' versus *samiʿa-hᵘ* 'he heard it', '*taqada-hᵘ* 'he believed it'.

stRRR is difficult to generalize about, because the number of roots in which it occurs is rather limited, but it includes verbs denoting tendencies, characteristics, mental evaluation and effort towards a state signalized by the primary stem—*staʿrabᵃ* 'he turned Arab', *stamātᵃ* 'he risked death'; *stadārᵃ* 'it was circular', *staqāmᵃ* 'it was straight', *staḥyā* 'he was shy'; *staḥsana-hᵘ* 'he approved of it', *staqbaḥa-hā* 'he thought her ugly (*qabīḥ*)'; *stafhamᵃ* 'he enquired' versus *fahima-hᵘ* 'he understood it'.

RūRR in many cases requires a personal direct object in contrast to another stem which is intransitive or requires a non-personal object—*kātaba-nī* 'he corresponded with me' versus *kataba-hᵘ* 'he wrote it', *ḥāwara-nī* 'he conversed with me' versus '*aḥāra jawāban* 'he returned an answer' and *ḥāra ljawābᵘ* 'the answer came back'.

RŘR is far and away most commonly used for generating denominative verbs (those which are derivative from a noun), but the implications of the verb are as unpredictable as they are in English denominative verbs—*qaṣṣara-hᵘ* 'he peeled it' implies that he removed the peel (*qišr*), whereas *jallada lkitāb* 'he bound the book' implies that he added a skin (*jild*) to it; *ʿabbara ʿan hāḏā lmaʿnā* 'he expressed this sentiment' is derived from the substantive *ʿibāra* 'mode of expression' and bears no easily traceable relationship to the primary stem verb *ʿabar*ᵃ 'he crossed'; *laqqabū-nā* 'they entitled us' is derived from *laqab* 'a title'; the stem can also be factitive, as in *ʿarraja-h*ᵘ 'he lamed him' versus *ʿarij*ᵃ 'he was lame', though it might be questioned whether this too is not really a denominative from *ʾaʿraj* 'lame'.[1]

RRR̄ is a stem only attested in verbs which match the type of noun described on p. 60, relating to colours and undesirable physical characteristics—*ḥmarr*ᵃ 'it was red', *ʿwajj*ᵃ 'it was crooked'.

tRv̄RR, if predicated of more than one entity, can depict their mutual interaction—*taqātalū* 'they fought together', *tabādarū* 'they raced each other', *tabādalū ttaḥiyyāt* 'they exchanged greetings'; the common statement that it depicts a pretence is a dubious generalization, and it would not be easy to find parallels for *taʿāmaytu* 'I turned a blind eye'; I suspect in fact that instances are a good deal commoner (though still limited in range) where it depicts a gradually phased process, as in *tasāqaṭa ddam* 'the blood dripped' versus *saqaṭa lḥajar* 'the stone dropped', *tamāšaynā* 'we strolled' versus *mašaynā* 'we walked', *talāšā* 'it faded away'.

tRR̄R is often an intransitive counterpart of the transitive value of another stem—*taḥarraka ššayʾ*ᵘ 'the thing moved' versus *ḥarraka ššayʾ*ᵃ 'he moved the thing', *tanawwara wajhu-hā* 'her face lit up' versus *nawwara lbayt*ᵃ 'it lit the house up', *taṣaddaʿat*ᵢ *ṣṣaḵra* 'the rock split' versus *ṣadaʿa ṣṣaḵra* 'he split the rock'; yet there are plenty of examples of transitive verbs of this stem, as *tabaṣṣara-nī* 'he gazed at me'.

In a good many cases two stems of a root are virtually synonymous: *jahara bi-h*ⁱ and *jāhara bi-h*ⁱ 'he declared it'.

Verb stems are productive in varying degrees. Least so are *nRRR* and *RRR̄*, whose available potentialities have already been fully exploited. But *RR̄R* and *stRRR* are still freely productive of new verbs: the former, by virtue of its denominative value, has been used to coin *ʾammam*ᵃ 'he nationalized (something)' on the basis of the substantive *ʾumma* 'a nation'; the latter stem has been employed for the coining of the participle *mustašriq* 'Orientalist' based on *ššarq* 'the Orient'. *tRv̄RR* is still potentially productive of verbs implying mutuality: an Arab would at once recognize *tajāsasū*, even if he had never heard it before (and it is not recorded in the dictionaries), as intended to mean 'they spied on each other'.

[1] The frequently repeated statement that this stem has an 'intensifying' value is, as a generalization, totally false. The two examples invariably quoted, *kassara-h*ᵘ 'he smashed it' versus *kasara-h*ᵘ 'he broke it' and *qattala-hum* 'he massacred them' versus *qatala-hum* 'he killed them' are rarities with hardly any parallel in the whole lexicon.

Verb sets

The total morphological varieties of the verb group into nine sets. Four of these are primary, and exhibit two-way contrasts each plotted in two dimensions. In one dimension, items which embody a specific agent pronoun contrast with items which are non-specific (in a sense explained below, p. 82); and the non-specific items are a complete mirror of all the specific items. In the other dimension, there are two contrasting sets, each one a counterpart of the other in containing thirteen items, matching the twelve items of the other pronoun sets (p. 39) plus a gender differentiation in regard to a duality of entities other than speaker and addressee(s).

Four secondary sets are merely syntactically determined variants of which two match the primary prefix set of the specific verb and two the primary prefix set of the non-specific verb. The ninth set, which conveys commands, is peripheral to the system.

The specific and the non-specific verb contrast morphologically only in their vowel-patterns. The two sets plotted in the other dimension contrast (i) in the shape of the predicate element, as mentioned above, p. 72, and (ii) in the agent pronoun morphemes, which differ not only as between one pronoun and another but also as between the two sets. In the 'suffix' set, the pronoun morphemes are exclusively suffixes, in the 'prefix' set they are discontinuous morphemes consisting of prefix and suffix. In the schematic tabulation on p. 77, the verb illustrated is the primary stem of the root *jls*, having the lexical value 'sit'.

The semantic contrast between suffix and prefix set lies in the value of the predicate element. This has little to do with the time contrasts which are generally felt in European languages to be a fundamental feature of the verb; very few Arabic verbs embody a wholly unambiguous time signal.

More important than time is a factor which can be called 'aspectual': this depends on whether the predicate is envisaged dynamically as depicting a change from one situation to another, or statically as depicting a single, ideally 'frozen', situation. What has been, in the previous section, called an event-stating predicate is dynamic, and has a necessary siting in time. All other types of predicate are static, and to these the time factor may or may not be relevant (p. 66); if it is considered relevant, it must be marked by other means than the morphology of the predicate verb, since static verb predicates are intrinsically non-time-marked, just as much as are non-verbal predicates (p. 67).

It is true that, with a predicate which is dominantly dynamic and event-stating, such as 'die', the suffix set verb unambiguously indicates past time. But the great majority of Arabic verbs are aspectually

	Speaker	Speaker with other(s)				
Suffix set	*jalas/t*^{u}	*jalas/nā*				
Prefix set	*'/ajlis/*^{u}	*n/ajlis/*^{u}				
	One male addressee	One female addressee	Two addressees	Plur. male addressees	Plur. female addressees	
Suffix set	*jalas/t*^{a}	*jalas/t*^{i}	*jalas/tumā*	*jalas/tum*	*jalas/tunna*	
Prefix set	*t/ajlis/*^{u}	*t/ajlis/īn*^{a}	*t/ajlis/ān*^{i}	*t/ajlis/ūn*^{a}	*t/ajlis/na*	
	Entities other than speaker(s) or addressee(s)					
	Masc. sing.	Fem. sing.	Masc. dual	Fem. dual	Masc. plur.	Fem. plur.
Suffix set	*jalas/*^{a}	*jalas/at*	*jalas/ā*	*jalas/atā*	*jalas/ū*	*jalas/na*
Prefix set	*y/ajlis/*^{u}	*t/ajlis/*^{u}	*y/ajlis/ān*^{i}	*t/ajlis/ān*^{i}	*y/ajlis /ūn*^{a}	*t/ajlis/na*

N.B. Certain modifications of the terminal elements of the prefix set, occasioned by the presence of a semivowel in the root, are more conveniently described in connection with the sub-varieties of that set, p. 83.

ambivalent, capable of being envisaged as either static or dynamic; an English rendering will often reflect this in a difference in the verb used:

Verbal abstract	Static value	Dynamic value
rukūb	'to ride'	'to mount'
ḥmirār	'to be red'	'to turn red'
'iqāma	'to reside'	'to settle'
ḥukm	'to govern'	'to decree'
'ilm	'to know'	'to get to know'

In these, only contextual considerations will determine the appropriate aspectual value, and in the case of static aspect, the time value.

A modifying functional *qad* transforms a suffix set item with dynamic aspect into one with static aspectual value, and hence no definite time marking. The unambiguously time-marked *mātat* 'she died' contrasts with *qad mātat* 'she is dead' or 'she was dead' (as in 'she was dead by the time I arrived'). In aspectually ambivalent verbs, however, the use of this functional is optional; taking three examples, the first being dynamic, the two others static,

(i) 'we knew the moment he opened his mouth that he was foreign'
(ii) 'we knew all along that he was foreign',
(iii) 'we know that the earth is round',

qad 'alimnā is appropriate only in the static predicates (ii) and (iii), but *'alimnā* unmodified is possible in all three sentences.

The prefix set is fundamentally static and non-time marked, taking its temporal coloration from the context. English so-called present tense forms cover three distinct concepts, all having a static aspect, and consequently all capable of being rendered by an Arabic prefix set verb. There is the generalized form of continuous validity, as in 'I love Mary' (the static nature of which can be appreciated by its congruity of sense with 'I am in love with Mary'), which can be rendered by the prefix set, or by the suffix set with static value: *'aḥbabtᵘ* and *qad 'aḥbabtᵘ* resemble *'alimnā* in their capability of depicting a past situation 'I loved/I was in love' as well as the generally valid one 'I love/I am in love', and the same is the case with the prefix set item *'uḥibbᵘ*; but there is a contrast with the unambiguous past time reference of *'aḥbabtᵘ* if this is used with the dynamic aspectual value 'I fell in love'. It is observable that some verbs with a dominantly static aspectual value (thus antithetical to dominantly dynamic verbs like 'die') are more commonly used in the suffix set than the prefix set—*fahimtᵘ* 'I understand', *karihtᵘ* 'I hate'. Secondly there is the form connoting a discontinuous series of events, such as 'I go to town every Tuesday', which is envisaged in Arabic as static because it describes a *pattern* of events rather than the events *per se*; the Arabic prefix set is normal for this. Thirdly, the form depicting a temporary situation coexisting with the moment of utterance, as in 'I am sitting in the garden'; this can be represented in SA either by a prefix set verb, or by a non-verbal theme + participle structure, *'ajlisᵘ* or *'ana jālis.*[1]

At another level of differentiation the suffix set predicates a fact, the prefix set a notional concept such as may have to be rendered in English by the use of an auxiliary like 'may', 'might', 'would', 'could', etc. 'He settled down in a corner where he could get a glimpse of the procession' demands in Arabic no functional of potentiality corresponding to 'could', for the prefix set item, with its notional value, sufficiently points the contrast with the factual event-predicate of '. . . where he got a glimpse' marked by the suffix set verb.

Since no statement relating to a time which lies in the future at the moment of utterance can be a known fact, it follows that the prefix set, with its 'notional' value, is appropriate for statements relating to futurity. If the speaker considers it desirable to mark explicitly the futurity of his proposition, he may use in addition the functional *sawfa* or *sa: sa-'ajlisᵘ* is explicitly 'I shall sit'. It has already been observed, however, that a future *event* can be denoted by the theme + participle structure (p. 70). The time value of this structure therefore depends on the aspectual value associated with the participle: if the verb which it matches is envisaged as having static value, the structure indicates the immediate situation coexisting with the moment of utterance, as mentioned above; if dynamic value is envisaged, it indicates a future event. Thus *lmaḥkamatu jālisa* can represent 'the court is (at the moment) in session' with static value, but will have dynamic and future value in the context 'the court will sit at 10.30 tomorrow to deliver sentence'.

The function of *qad* when used in conjunction with a prefix set item is to stress two of the potential values of that set, either its use to denote a recurring pattern, or its use with the value of possibility or probability: *qad nubṣiru hāḏā* 'we may frequently observe this', *qad yamūtu ṭṭifl* 'the child may well die'.

From all the above, it emerges that the only definitely time-marked verb (unless time-marked by a modifying functional or an adverbial) is the suffix set verb in cases where it has dynamic aspect, being then explicitly past. The lack of significance of the time factor is particularly noticeable in subordinate clauses, where the time is sufficiently marked by the main predicate. Whereas in English one cannot avoid two past-time marked predicates in 'he dropped the knife which he was holding', it is perfectly possible in Arabic to use a non-time marked predicate (non-verbal or prefix set verb) for the second.

[1] The theme + participle structure is practically universal in the vernaculars for this sense, and the use of the prefix set verb consequently has something of a 'literary' flavour.

Modifying verbs

Where the time factor is considered relevant to a static predicate, this is marked by the use of a modifying verb with root *kwn*. This possesses the full normal repertory of suffix and prefix set items. Its suffix set serves to mark explicitly past time, its prefix set future time or notional value. It modifies either a simple non-verbal predicate structure, or a clause structure containing the verb which conveys the main predicate. Its use entails some structural transformations of the sentence:

(i) the theme of the unmodified sentence becomes the agent of *kwn*;
(ii) a simple noun-predicate of the unmodified sentence exchanges its mark of independent status for that of subordinate status;
(iii) the substantive or demonstrative agent of an unmodified verbal sentence structure normally becomes the agent of *kwn* (and commonly placed immediately after it, though instances can be observed where it retains its original position after the main predicate verb);
(iv) the pronoun agent of a verb in the unmodified structure is repeated both in the modifying verb and in the main verb if it is in fact identical with the theme of the whole sentence;
(v) in so far as not affected by the above-mentioned points, a clause predicate retains its original structure.

These points can be illustrated as follows:

Unmodified structure	Structure modified by suffix set of *kwn*
'ana fī bārīs 'I am in Paris'	*kuntu fī bārīs* (i) 'I was in Paris'
hum ṣaḥafiyyūn 'they are journalists'	*kānū ṣaḥafiyyīn* (i, ii) 'they were journalists'
tajlisu lmaḥkamatu kulla yawm 'the court sits daily'	*kānat*$_i$ *lmaḥkamatu tajlisu kulla yawm* (iii) 'the court used to sit daily'
karihtu hāḏā l'amal 'I hate this job'	*kuntu karihtu hāḏā l'amal* (iv) 'I hated this job'
hāḏihi l'ibāratu ma'nā-hā wāḍiḥun li-lmudarris ⟨this expression, its meaning is obvious to the teacher⟩ 'the meaning of this expression is obvious to the teacher'	*kānat hāḏihi l'ibāratu ma'nā-hā wāḍiḥun li-lmudarris* (i, v) 'the meaning of this expression was obvious to the teacher'

lbintu qad māta wālidā-hā mun ḏu sana
⟨the girl, have been dead her parents since a year⟩
'the girl's parents have been dead for a year'

kānat$_i$ *lbintu qad māta wālidā-hā munḏu sana* (i, v)
'the girl's parents had died a year previously'

Of course, further extrapolation of the term functioning as agent of *kwn* into a theme placed before it is possible, and necessary if the total sentence is introduced by a functional demanding a thematic sentence structure. The replacement of the suffix set item of *kwn*, illustrated above, by a corresponding prefix set item entails substitution of 'will/would/might/could/etc. be' for the past time indications in the renderings given, but in no way changes the structures.

Alongside *kwn*, there is a series of other modifying verbs[1] which behave structurally in exactly the same way, but embody an additional semantic modification such as 'almost', 'begin', 'continue', etc. As with *kwn*, it is the modifying verb which performs the task of marking time or the fact-versus-notion contrast. Thus, *'abkī* 'I cry', *kuntu 'abkī* 'I used to cry', *kidtu 'abkī* 'I nearly cried', *ẓaliltu 'abkī* 'I went on crying', *jaʿaltu 'abkī* 'I began crying', *sawfa 'aʿūdu 'abkī* 'I shall cry again'.

The time, or notional, indication provided by a modifying verb need not be repeated in a series of coordinate predicates, since the initial occurrence of the modifier suffices as a context to determine the value of the succeeding predicates: *kuntu 'uġādiru lbayta kulla ṣabāḥin wa-'uġalliqu lbāba ḵalf-ī* 'I left the house every morning and

[1] The modifying verbs were originally autonomous predicates, but to a large extent have lost this potentiality in SA. Only a handful are still capable of either use, such as *dwm*, in *dāmat ḥurūbun taštaʿil* 'wars raged continuously' as well as *dāmat ḥurūb* 'wars continued'. It may be remarked of *kwn* that it is now almost never used autonomously. The static autonomous value 'exist' is expressed by patterns of the root *wjd* (*wujid*^{a}, *yūjad*, and the verbal abstract *wujūd*); the dynamic autonomous value of 'coming into being' was expressed in medieval philosophy by the verbal abstract *kawn*, but this tends in SA to be replaced by *takawwun*.

Some of the modifying verbs of SA were in ancient Arabic autonomous predicates with a time-locatory significance, e.g. *lammā 'aṣbaḥnā* ⟨when we were in the morning⟩ 'when morning had dawned on us'. But the amplification of such a predicate by an additional adverbial phrase opens the way for a new structural analysis whereby the addition is felt to contain the main predicate and the verb to be a modifier of it: *'aṣbaḥnā fī makka* will have evolved from ⟨we morninged in Mecca⟩ (as in English 'we wintered in Nice') towards 'by the morning, we were in Mecca'. The latter analysis then came to preponderate, and the (now) modifying verb assumed the value of 'come to be . . .' with every kind of main predicate; yet in early medieval Arabic some feeling for the time value remained, so that a difference was still perceptible between *'aṣbaḥnā* 'by the morning, we came to be . . .' and *'amsaynā* 'by the evening, we came to be . . .' and the choice of one or other was dictated by appropriateness to the context, albeit such appropriateness was mostly metaphorical and not literal. In SA, these verbs have practically lost all time significance and can be used indifferently for 'become . . .'

locked the door behind me', where the prefix set item *'uğalliqu* 'I (habitually) lock' is signalized as having past time relevance by the modifier *kuntu* at the beginning of the previous sentence.

When an identificatory predicate has a modifying verb, the pronominal secondary theme (p. 68) may be reduced to the status of a predicate-marking functional: *kāna lʿarabu hum$_u$ lğālibūn* 'the Arabs were the victors' has the predicate term marked for independent status as simple predicate of the secondary theme *hum*; but an alternative is . . . *lğālibīn* marked for subordinate status as predicate of *kāna* (p. 80, ii), so that *hum* no longer has thematic status.

The non-specific verb

Mention has been made of the two-dimensional extension of the verb system, and one dimension has been described which shows the contrast between suffix and prefix sets. Parallel to these, and marked by identical pronoun morphemes, are two primary sets contrasting morphologically with the former by a distinctive vowel pattern for the predicate element, the pattern here being uniformly *u–i* in the suffix set and *u–a* in the prefix set, in all stems. Thus, using for illustration the primary stem and two of the secondary stems,

	Specific	Non-specific
Suffix	$R_1aR_2vR_3$/ $staR_1R_2aR_3$/ $R_1\bar{a}R_2aR_3$/	$R_1uR_2iR_3$/ $stuR_1R_2iR_3$/ $R_1\bar{u}R_2iR_3$/
Prefix	/$aR_1R_2vR_3$/ /$astaR_1R_2iR_3$/ /$uR_1\bar{a}R_2iR_3$/	/$uR_1R_2aR_3$/ /$ustaR_1R_2aR_3$/ /$uR_1\bar{a}R_2aR_3$/

The function of the non-specific sets is to neutralize the specificity of the agent term. In the verb as hitherto described, the non-predicate element has been a known and specifically recognizable entity. The non-specific verb eliminates this specification in favour of an agent which is vaguely 'somebody' or 'something'. But structurally, a direct[1] object of the specific verb moves into the position of a pseudo-agent of the non-specific verb: specific *'aḵbarat-nī* 'she told me' contrasts with *'uḵbirtu* 'somebody told me/I was told by somebody'. The real agent of the non-specific verb is usually unspecified[2]; Arabic has no need of

[1] See below, p. 87, on this term.

[2] It is an open question whether *min qibali*, which corresponds roughly to 'de la part de', can be said to mark the real agent after a verb of this kind. Though used in SA in contexts where English would use the passive + 'by' structure, it is wider in implication: *qad 'ursila min qibali-nā* 'il a été envoyé de notre part' can, but does not necessarily, imply that 'we' were the actual despatchers.

the inversion form of English 'the victors built the mosque' versus 'the mosque was built by the victors', because the differentiation conveyed by those two English forms is effected simply by extrapolating the appropriate entity as theme, ⟨the victors, they-built the mosque⟩ versus ⟨the mosque, built-it the victors⟩.

The specific verb which needs a preposition with its object is matched by a non-specific verb having a morphological shape identical with that implying a mas. sing. pronoun agent: specific *raḍiyat ʿan-hum* 'she was satisfied with them' is matched by non-specific *ruḍiya ʿan-hum* ⟨somebody was satisfied with them⟩ 'satisfaction was felt with them'.

The verbal abstract, since it is in itself devoid of allusion to an agent, subsumes both the specific and the non-specific implications of the English 'infinitive'; Arabic has no overt distinction between 'to murder' and 'to be murdered'. Nor is this made clear even if the verbal abstract is annexed to a single amplifying entity: *qatl-ī* 'my murder' covers both 'my murdering (someone else)' and 'my being murdered'. The differentiation only becomes clear if the annexion is replaced by a preposition (p. 47), since the preposition differs according to whether the entity following it has the status of agent or object.

Participles have two varieties (cp. p. 73) matching the two kinds of verb. The participle pattern *kātib* matches the specific *yaktub* 'he writes' and has the value 'a person who writes/a writer'; the pattern *maktūb* matches the non-specific *yuktab* 'somebody writes it/it is written' and has the value 'a thing which somebody writes/something in writing'.

Syntactically determined variations in the verb

The two primary prefix sets, specific and non-specific, have each two additional variations determined by the syntactic context. Morphologically, these are marked by changes in the termination of the word, and the changes are of such a nature that they could be conveniently designated the *a*-subset and the 'short' subset, these being the most general characteristics of the patterns:

	Primary set	*a*-subset	short subset
All verbs other than of types listed below	$/^{u}$	$/^{a}$	/zero
R_2 = semivowel	$/R_1\bar{v}R_3{}^{u}$	$/R_1\bar{v}R_3{}^{a}$	$/R_1vR_3$
$R_3 = w$ and preceded by *u*	$/R_2\bar{u}$	$/R_2uwa$	$/R_2u$
$R_3 = y$ and preceded by *i*	$/R_2\bar{\imath}$	$/R_2iya$	$/R_2i$
$R_3 = w/y$ preceded by *a*	$/R_2\bar{a}$		$/R_2a$

But in those items where the pronoun morpheme includes a terminal *-ūn*^{i} or *-ūn*^{a}, the *a*-subset and the short subset are uniformly differentiated from the primary set simply by elimination of the *n*^{i}/*n*^{a}.

The functional *'an* + prefix set (p. 56) demands the *a*-subset of the latter. Certain other functionals, such as *li* 'in order that' also demand it. But it is those specific functionals, and only those, which occasion its use. It is therefore unlike a Latin subjunctive, as can be seen from the contrast between *ṭalabū malja'an li-yak̲tabi'ū* 'they sought for a refuge in order that they might hide' and *ṭalabū malja'an ḥayt̲u yak̲tabi'ūn*^{a} 'they sought for a refuge where they might hide', since 'where' is not a functional requiring the use of the subset.

By far the commonest occurrence of the short subset is after the negative functional *lam* (p. 99), though there are some other syntactic situations which also demand it (below and p. 105).

Commands, etc.

The command is visualized as a direct address to the hearer calling for action on his part. This has four consequences: pronoun differentiation becomes irrelevant to the extent that the only possible agent of a command verb is the person(s) addressed; the non-specific reflex is excluded; command verbs always have dynamic aspect; and prohibitions (which call for abstention from action) are not visualized as commands and have a different structure.

Morphologically, the command verb resembles the short variety of the prefix set of a specific verb, minus the first syllable which contains the marks of pronoun differentiation; it retains, however, the markers which differentiate the gender and number of the hearer(s). 'Sit down!' is *jlis* addressed to one male, *jlisū* addressed to a plurality of males, etc.

The dynamic aspect of a command may be formally obscured: *kun ma'a-nā* ⟨be with us⟩ in fact has the dynamic value 'accompany us' or 'join us'.

Exhortations or aspirations of the type expressed by English 'let us go', 'let them consider this', use the short variety of the prefix set, with pronoun differentiation, and signalized by a distinctive functional *l* which is almost always accompanied in SA by the coordinating functional *wa* 'and' or by *fa* which may either have coordinating function (p. 97) or be a purely mechanical accompaniment of the *l*: *fa-l-najlis* 'let's sit down then'. In theory, if *wa* or *fa* does not precede, the exhortatory functional should have the form *li*, but this hardly ever occurs in SA.

Prohibitions together with negative exhortations have a uniform structure: short variety of the prefix set with negative functional (see further p. 99).

Conclusion

The following synopsis of a passage from M. A. Enan's *Decisive moments in the history of Islam* (Cairo, 1962, pp. 72–3) may be useful in illustrating some of the ways in which the Arabic verb system works:

'In A.D. 774, S. and H. revolted [1] and made a pact [2] to wage war on A.; the fact of A.'s being otherwise preoccupied was [3] a thing which encouraged [4] these rebels. A. decided [5] that he should hasten [6] to repress them, so he sent [7] an army, but S. routed [8] it and it dispersed [9]. The revolt became stronger [10]. The rebels, at whose head was [11] S., were not content [12] with this success, because of what they knew [13] of A.'s determination. They got the idea [14] of calling the king of the Franks to aid. S., whom the Latin tradition calls [15] B., marched [16] in spring A.D. 777 to meet Charlemagne; the latter was residing [17] at that time in Paderborn and was at the moment disengaged [18] after defeating the Saxons, and he began organizing [19] aid for them'.

fa-fī sanati 774 ***ṯāra*** [1] *sulaymānu wa-lḥusaynu wa-**taḥālafā*** [2] *ʿalā muḥārabati ʿabdi rraḥmāni wa-**kāna*** [3] *nšiġālu ʿabdi rraḥmāni mim-mā **yušajjiʿu*** [4] *ʾulāʾika lḵawārija, wa-**raʾā*** [5] *ʿabdu rraḥmāni ʾan **yubādira*** [6] *ʾilā mudāfaʿati-him fa-**ʾarsala*** [7] *jayšan fa-**hazama**-hū* [8] *sulaymānu wa-**tafarraqa*** [9], *wa-**stafḥala*** [10] *ʾamru ṯṯawrati, walākinna zuʿamāʾa ṯṯawrati wa-**ʿalā raʾsi-him** sulaymānu* [11] ***lam yaṭmaʾinnū*** [12] *ʾilā ḏālika nnaṣri li-mā **yaʿlamūna**-hū* [13] *min ʿazmi ʿabdi rraḥmāni, fa-**fakkarū*** [14] *fī lʾintiṣāri bi-maliki lfaranji wa-**sāra*** [16] *sulaymānu wa-**tusammīhi*** [15] *rriwāyatu llātīniyyatu bnaIʾaʿrābiyyi ʾilā liqāʾi šāralamāna fī rabīʿi sanati* 777, *wa-**kāna** yawmaʾiḏin **yuqīmu*** [17] *balāṭa-hū fī madīnati Bāderbūrun wa-**kāna qad fariġa*** [18] *yawmaʾiḏin min hazīmati ssaksūniyyīna wa-**ʾaḵaḏa yunaẓẓimu*** [19] *tanṣīra-hum.*

Bold type in this passage signalizes the predicates. The following are explanatory notes on the predicate structures.

[1] Suffix set item of verb, with dynamic aspect, marking past event.

[2] *tRv̄RR* stem implying mutuality; suffix set item as in [1].

[3] suffix set item of the modifying verb *kwn*, assigning past time relevance to an intrinsically non-time-marked classificatory predicate.

[4] *RR̄R* stem, prefix set item with static aspect and classificatory value, thus corresponding to 'was an encouragement' rather than the dynamic 'encouraged' which seems natural in English; being static and classificatory it is not time-marked, the past time relevance being sufficiently clear from the time-marking of the main predicate [3].

[5] suffix set item with dynamic aspect, as past event.

[6] *RvRR* stem, prefix set item with notional value, in the *a*-subset as demanded by the presence of the functional *'an* 'that'.

[7], [8] suffix set items as [1].

[9] *tRRR* stem with intransitive force contrasting with transitive *farraqa-hū* 'he dispersed it', suffix set item as [1].

[10] *stRRR* stem denoting a characteristic, suffix set item with dynamic aspect thus implying the coming into possession of the characteristic.

[11] locatory predicate structure with no verb and no time indication and here placed in front of the clause theme *sulaymānu.*

[12] negative reflex (*lam* + short subset item of the prefix set) of the *qad* + suffix set structure (see p. 99), having static aspect and no intrinsic time indication; taken out of the present context it could equally well have represented 'are not content'.

[13] prefix set item with static aspect and hence ambiguous as to time in the same way as [12].

[14] *RR̄R* stem denominative of the substantive *fikra* 'idea'; here with dynamic aspect in the suffix set item as a past event; the static aspectual value of this verb is 'think'.

[15] *RR̄R* stem denominative from *sm* 'a name'; prefix set item as a generalized statement of continuous validity.

[16] suffix set item with dynamic aspect.

[17] the main predicate is an *'RRR* stem with static aspectual value, contrasting with the dynamic value 'settle', in the prefix set item, and not in itself time-marked, but given past time relevance by the addition of the suffix set item of the modifying verb *kwn.*

[18] the main predicate is a suffix set item marked as having static aspect by *qad*, and to that extent ambiguous as to time (admitting either 'he was disengaged' or 'he is disengaged'), but marked for past time by the addition of the modifying verb *kwn.*

[19] prefix set item of the main predicate verb 'organize', with suffix set item of the modifying verb *'ak̲ad̲a* which both marks the past time and adds the modifying concept 'begin'.

Predicates 4, 11, 12 and 13, which in English are necessarily time-marked, have in the Arabic no time indication at all apart from the general context in which they are placed. 1, which precedes a duality of agents, is not number-marked, but 2, referring back to them, has the dual marking *-ā* (p. 72). 15 is incorporated in an English 'relative' clause, but in Arabic is coordinately structured, cp. p. 50; so too 11 is not in an adjectival clause, as the English is, but in a circumstantial one (p. 90).

11

AMPLIFICATION OF THE PREDICATE

The term 'adverbial' is strictly speaking inappropriate for Arabic, because the function which one needs to describe is that of amplifying a predicate, irrespective of whether the latter be expressed with or without a verb. But if this is allowed for, the term has a practical usefulness in distinguishing two kinds of amplification, the 'object' and the 'adverbial'.

An adverbial is an amplification which can be deleted from the sentence without impairing the viability of the predicate. The predicate of 'he died' is viable without any amplifications such as 'yesterday', 'in my arms', 'a lingering death' or 'laughing'. But some predicates are incomplete without amplification: 'murder' is significant only if there is a person murdered as well as a murderer, 'peruse' only if there is something perused as well as a peruser. Amplifications required by the nature of the predicate are 'objects': indirect if signalled by a preposition, direct if not so signalled.

In Arabic, amplifications of both kinds will be found marked either by the morpheme of subordinate status (unless neutralized), or by a preposition. *'asqaṭa lkitāba ʿalā rijl-ī* 'he dropped the book on my foot' shows the object 'book' marked by the morpheme of subordinate status and the adverbial by the preposition *ʿalā*; but *ṭṭalaʿa ʿalā lkitābi yawma l'aḥad* 'he perused the book on Sunday' shows the reverse arrangement, with indirect object and the adverbial marked as having subordinate status.

A preposition which marks the indirect object has to be regarded as part of the predicate lexeme: 'he perused' is *ṭṭalaʿa ʿalā* and not *ṭṭalaʿ*[a], rather as in English 'look over' in 'look over the document' is a different lexeme from 'look' in 'look over the wall'.

A point of practical importance in the distinction between an object and an adverbial is that of word order: briefly, an adverbial can precede the predicate, an object normally cannot.

It is not easy to establish for Arabic a clearly defined word class of prepositions: most of its items seem to have been originally substantives marked as adverbial by the marker of subordinate status (and there are even today borderline cases). A clear indication of this is that the substantive placed after a preposition carries the marker of dependent status just as it does after an annexed substantive. Contrast for example *māta qabla fušuwwi ṭṭāʿūn* 'he died before the outbreak of the plague' with *māta sanata fušuwwi ṭṭāʿūn* 'he died the year of the outbreak of the plague': these are identically structured, with verb + adverbial marked as having subordinate status + substantive marked as having dependent status; consequently *qabla* has the same structural status as *sanata* 'year' and could be evaluated as a substantive with the value 'antecedent period'.

A good many concepts which in English receive expression by prepositions are rendered in Arabic by adverbially marked substantives which retain the potentiality of functioning in independent position: the Arabic for 'he hid behind the woodshed' exhibits the same structure as dialectal English 'he hid back of the woodshed', and 'back' remains capable of functioning as a theme, as in 'the back of the woodshed is rotten'. And one could contrast its prepositional use as a locatory predicate 'this is behind [with marker of subordinate status] the woodshed' with its use as a substantival identificatory predicate 'this is the back [with marker of independent status] of the woodshed'.

There is also a group of words which, although they have lost their capability of functioning in independent position, still show some substantival characteristics: *ʿinda lqāḍī* 'with (chez) the judge' changes its marker of subordinate status into that of dependent status when placed after a preposition as in *min ʿindi lqāḍī* 'from the judge's presence'; *maʿa* 'together with', if used adverbially in the sense of 'together' and without a following substantive, appears as *maʿan* with the terminal *-n* characteristic of substantives not annexed (p. 52).

Yet another group, though functioning in all attested Arabic exclusively as prepositions, may well be historically speaking fossilized substantives, such as *ʿalā* 'on', which could originally have been 'top of' (like 'back of' cited above). Only three prepositions, with minimal phonetic shape of consonant + short vowel, namely *bi* 'in/by', *li* 'for', *ka* 'as', wholly resist such an interpretation.

There are very few Arabic words which function exclusively as adverbials. Here again, some of them are merely fossilized substantives which have shed their function as such with or without morphological change. Within the historical period this change has taken place with SA *'ams*^{i} 'yesterday' (adverbial only), which does not occur in the Qur'ān, where it is represented by a preposition + substantive phrase *bi-l'ams*^{i} 'on the eve'. It is true that the words for 'here' and 'there' are constructed on the morphological plane solely out of deictic elements and do not function otherwise than as equivalent to a prepositional phrase 'in this/that place'; but in contrast, *l'ān*^{a} 'now' is a substantive capable of functioning otherwise than adverbially, as in *'ilā l'ān*^{i} 'up to the present' and *jā'a l'ān*^{u} 'the time has come'.

Arabic has no word class corresponding to English adverbs of the *-ly* type. In so far as these amplify a predicate, they may be expressed by a substantive marked as adverbial[1] either by the marker of subordinate status or by a preposition: 'he laughed softly' can be expressed as *ḍaḥika ḍaḥkan hādi'an* 'he laughed a soft laugh', or *ḍaḥika hādi'an* ⟨he laughed a soft thing⟩, or *ḍaḥika bi-ṣawtin hādi'*^{in} 'he laughed in a soft tone'; 'he died very horribly' as *māta 'ašna'a mawt*^{in} 'he died the most horrible death'. In some cases the English adverbial concept is embodied in the Arabic verb, and the English predicate in an object term, as in *'asra'ū mašya-hum* ⟨they hastened their walk⟩ 'they walked hastily'.

English *-ly* adverbs which amplify an adjective are structured in Arabic as adjectives annexed to a substantive embodying the concept of the English adjective: 'bitterly hostile' as ⟨bitter of hostility⟩ (p. 47).

Circumstantial clauses

It is hardly necessary to do more here than allude to the existence of clauses marked as adverbials of time, causation, etc., by appropriate functional markers ('when he came', 'because he came', etc.); further discussion of them will be found in Chapter 13. But the circumstantial clause presents features of interest.

This is the case of a proposition which is presented merely as an attendant circumstance to the main predicate. The logical relationship between the main proposition and the circumstantial one is highly variable: the circumstantial clause may be purely temporal, or adversative (implying something unexpected in the simultaneous validity of the two propositions), or explanatory (implying that the clause affords a reason for the main proposition). But there is an unsophisticated lack of overt marks of the logical intention.

One structure of this kind has a clause form preceded by a functional *wa*, which must have been originally the ordinary coordinating functional 'and': just as in English we find 'he has behaved disgracefully

[1] Words and phrases of this kind are true adverbials in the sense of the definition given at the beginning of this chapter and not 'objects'; although they are what I have, in *Written Arabic*, termed 'internal objects'.

to me, and he calls himself my friend', where the implied logical relationship is adversative, i.e. 'and' is replaceable by 'although'. But in medieval and SA, the circumstantial *wa* has come to be felt as having its own clearly defined functional value, although still logically ambiguous to the extent of admitting temporal ('while'), adversative ('although') and causal ('inasmuch as') interpretations. A clause marked by the circumstantial *wa* is always presented as aspectually static and structured either thematically, or verbally with a suffix set verb, and in the latter case the verb is in SA (though not necessarily in Quranic Arabic) preceded by the static aspect marker *qad* (p. 78).

Since the circumstantial *wa* has acquired its own functional status, a clause so marked can now be emboxed within the structure of the main proposition, which could hardly have been possible while it was still felt as a coordinator. Such a clause can moreover be placed in front of the main proposition, thereby functioning logically as a theme, as other adverbials can (p. 64); but since such a placing would of itself lead to misapprehension of the function of the *wa*, which would look like a coordinator, this can only be done if the theme-marking functional *'ammā* (p. 65) is also used, thus *'ammā wa-qad māta mukbir-ī fa-'ukbiru-ka bi-lqiṣṣa* 'now that my informant is dead, I can tell you the story' (logical relationship being here causal).

In a second type of circumstantial structure, the clause begins with a prefix set verb, but has no functional marker. Here again, the distinctiveness of the circumstantial function can have been hardly felt in ancient Arabic, because such a structure did not necessarily differ from that of an amplifying clause, which also *might* lack a functional marker (p. 50). But as soon as the rule had developed that a clause amplifying a defined substantive must be marked by an item of the *lladī* set, then the *absence* of the latter marker after a defined substantive and before a prefix set verb came to indicate distinctly the circumstantial function of the verb. So there is a contrast between *ramā ṭṭā'ira lladī yajṭimu fī l'arḍ* 'he shot the bird which was sitting on the ground' (amplifying structure, distinguishing the shot bird from others which were flying) and *ramā ṭṭā'ira yajṭimu fī l'arḍ* 'he shot the bird while it was sitting on the ground' (circumstantial structure, implying 'and not while that same bird was on the wing'). It will be observed of course that there is still some ambiguity about the case where the preceding substantive is undefined, *ramā ṭā'iran yajṭimu fī l'arḍ* 'he shot a bird sitting on the ground'; the grammarians insist that the clause is then adjectival and not circumstantial, a dogma which enables them to posit the convenient rule of thumb that a substantive whose situation is described by a circumstantial clause is always defined. The dogma is tenable if we are prepared also to stipulate that lack of definition of an entity precludes the hearer from considering its possible differences of situation. But it would perhaps be truer to say that indefinition of an entity neutralizes the functional contrast between amplifying clause and circumstantial clause, and that the structure then subsumes both functions. A structure such as *daḵala šayḵun yalbasu ṯawban 'aswad* 'a sheikh wearing a black robe came in', is purely neutral in respect of any differentiation between whether he happened at that particular moment to be wearing black, or whether he always wore black.

The prefix set verb used circumstantially has, in addition to the logical values already detailed, also that of denoting a purpose: *ḵaraja l'amīru yarmī* 'the emir went out shooting' does not imply that he was shooting at the moment of his emergence, but that he went out with the intention of shooting. In this connection the requirement for the entity described by the clause to be defined assumes a real functional value: for *daḵala ššayḵu yalbasu ṯawban aswad* is capable of being interpreted as 'the sheikh came in in order to don a black robe', but the substitution of *šayḵun* would not admit of this.

Finally, it may be mentioned that although in a large number of cases the circumstantial clause describes the situation of an entity figuring in the main sentence, this is not necessarily so: *waṣala lqaryata wa-lqamaru ṭāliʿ* 'he reached the village when the moon was rising'.

12

CLAUSE CONVERSION

Substantive clauses

In principle, any substantive clause whatever can be restructured around a verbal abstract. This procedure neutralizes the contrast between a factual and a notional substantive clause (p. 56) since 'his arrival' covers both 'the fact of his having arrived' and 'the possibility, etc., that he may arrive': compare e.g. 'his arrival yesterday has upset my plans' with 'his arrival tomorrow may upset my plans'. In spite of this, the verbal abstract formulation is extensively employed, even in quite elaborate structures. Indeed, it is virtually mandatory in the position of theme, since there is a considerable reluctance to beginning a sentence with an *'an* or *'anna* clause. 'The fact that he gave me some money does not prevent me speaking my mind' would normally be phrased as 'his giving me some money . . .' unless of course the sentence is structured verbally as ⟨not prevents-me speaking my mind the fact that he gave . . .⟩.

A substantive clause with verb predicate occasions no difficulty in conversion. The facilities of the annexion structure and of prepositional amplification of the verbal abstract (p. 83) afford ample scope for fitting in all the entities figuring in the clause structure. But in addition to these facilities, a verbal abstract can even, if necessary, retain the agent and direct object of the verb with their original syntactic markings, though admittedly this is decidedly unusual in SA in the case of the agent; but a modern historian can write *ʿtināq*^{v} *lmuslimīna nnaṣrāniyya*^{ta} 'the embracing of Christianity by the Muslims', where 'Muslims' is marked for dependent status being in agent relationship to the verbal abstract which is annexed to it (p. 46), while 'Christianity' retains the marker of subordinate status which it would have had after the verb as direct object. The writer could, of course, have equally well, had he chosen, replaced the direct object term by the prepositional substitution (p. 47) *li-nnaṣrāniyya*^{ti}.

When the substantive clause has a non-verbal predicate, the conversion structure uses the verbal abstract of *kwn*, which is *kawn: 'anna-hu fī lmadīna* 'the fact that he is in the city' converts to *kawn*^{v}*-hu fī lmadīna* 'his being in the city'.

Clauses containing any modifying verb convert by transforming the modifying verb into its verbal abstract, leaving the main predicate unaltered. Hence *'an yakūna fī lmadīna* '(the possibility) that he may be in the city' also converts to *kawn*^{v}*-hu fī lmadīna*. Similarly:

'ann-ī kuntu 'abkī	'the fact that I was crying'	*kawn-ī 'abkī*
'an 'akūna 'abkī	'the possibility that I may be crying'	
'ann-ī kuntu qad waṣalt^{u}	'the fact that I had arrived'	*kawn-ī qad waṣalt*^{u}
'an 'akūna qad waṣalt^{u}	'the possibility that I may have arrived'	
'annī dumtu 'abkī	'the fact that I incessantly cried'	*dawām-ī 'abkī*
'an 'adūma 'abkī	'the possibility that I may go on crying'	
'ann-ī dumtu ğaniyyan	'the fact that I was still rich'	*dawām-ī ğaniyyan*
'an 'adūma ğaniyyan	'the possibility that I may still be rich'	

When a substantive clause functions as direct object of a verb connoting mental activity (including 'see' where this is mental and not physical), conversion to the verbal abstract structure is rare, but there is instead another common type of conversion, in which the theme of the clause becomes the direct object of the main verb, the predicate remaining unaltered except that a non-verbal noun predicate exchanges its marker of independent status for that of subordinate status:

ʿalimtu 'anna-ka ʿalā ṣṣawāb *ʿalimtu-ka ʿalā ṣṣawāb*
'I know you are in the right'

ʿtaqadtu 'anna ššayḵa muḵṭi'^{un} *ʿtaqadtu ššayḵa muḵṭi'an*
'I believe the sheikh is mistaken'

ʿtaqadtu ʾanna-hum yukṭiʾūnᵃ *ʿtaqadtu-hum yukṭiʾūnᵃ*
'I believe they are making a mistake'

ʾaḥtamilu ʾanna-hā qad waṣalat *ʾaḥtamilu-hā qad waṣalat*
'I suppose she has arrived'

But in the case of a notional substantive clause marked by *ʾan* + the *a*-subset of the prefix verb (p. 84), the verb reverts to its primary form with the disappearance of the *ʾan* which is the sole reason for the use of the subset:

ʾarjū ʾan yajīʾū *ʾarjū-hum yajīʾūnᵃ*
'I hope they may come'

Adjectival clauses

English is familiar with the conversion of an adjectival clause into a participle, provided that the theme of the clause is identical with the amplified substantive, 'a parson who hunts' being convertible into 'a hunting parson'. This limitation does not exist in Arabic, though there are two types of clause structure which are not convertible: that with a pronoun theme other than the amplified entity (*buqʿatᵛ ʾuḥibbu-hā* 'a land which I love'), and that with a non-verbal structure consisting of entity term and locatory phrase (*buqʿatᵛ fī-hā ʾusūd* 'a land in which lions are').

In order to appreciate the somewhat remarkable features of the Arabic conversion structure, it is best to consider a triangular diagram of clause with verb predicate, clause with noun predicate, and the conversion structure. A phrase which can only be expressed in English as 'in a land whose kings are powerful' has three possible formulations in Arabic:

(i) clause with verb predicate (ii) clause with noun predicate
fī buqʿatin yaʿtazzu mulūku-hā *fī buqʿatin mulūku-hā muʿtazzūnᵃ*

(iii) conversion structure
fī buqʿatin muʿtazzin mulūku-hā

The points to be noticed in this are:

(a) in all three formulations the theme of the clause, *mulūku* 'kings', retains its syntactic marking of independent status appropriate to a theme;

(b) (iii) resembles (ii) in that the term 'powerful' is expressed by the participle pattern *muʿtazz*, and in that this is in the masculine form appropriate to 'kings'; but it contrasts with (ii) in that *muʿtazz* has exchanged its syntactic marker of independent status appropriate to the function of predicate for the syntactic marker matching that of *buqʿatin* 'land' to which it is now an adjective;

(c) the numerical marking of *muʿtazz* in (iii) resembles that of *yaʿtazzu* in (i) (which is singular according to the principle stated p. 72).

The conversion participle must also, as an adjective, match the amplified entity in definitional status, hence: *fī lbuqʿati lmuʿtazzi mulūku-hā* 'in the country whose kings are powerful'.

In have laid some stress on the syntactic markings because of their oddity to European feeling, but the word order (plus in suitable cases the gender marking of the conversion participle, which matches that of the clause theme and not that of the amplified entity) is quite sufficient to make the conversion structure clearly recognizable, even if *'iʿrāb* were to be discarded, as in *fī buqʿa muʿtazz mulūk-hā* which contrasts with the word order of (ii).

A clause amplifying an item of the *llaḏī* set used substantivally (p. 49) converts into a phrase with defined participle functioning substantivally, and syntactically marked according to its position in the sentence. The English phrase 'for the sake of the person/thing of whom/which mention has occurred previously' has the Arabic formulations:

(i) *li-'ajli llaḏī sabaqa ḏikru-h*^{u} (ii) *li-'ajli llaḏī ḏikru-hu sābiq*^{un}
(iii) *li-'ajli ssābiqi ḏikru-h*^{u}

A clause embodying a non-specific verb predicate converts on the same lines. The pseudo-agent retains its morpheme of independent status and is matched in gender by the participle in the conversion structure; when the clause has an indirect real object, the participle in the conversion structure is, like the verb in the clause, formally masculine singular:

li-mra'atin qutila wālidā-hā *li-mra'atin maqtūlin wālidā-hā*
'for a woman whose parents were murdered'

li-mra'atin 'ušīra 'ilay-hā *li-mra'atin mušārin 'ilay-hā*
'for a woman to whom reference has been made'

Circumstantial clauses

These are convertible on the same lines as adjectival clauses. But to the limitations on the possibility of conversion mentioned above, it must be added that circumstantial clauses are not convertible if they do not describe the situation of any entity mentioned in the main sentence. Structurally, the conversion differs from that of an adjectival clause only in that the term representing the clause-predicate uniformly shows the syntactic marker of subordinate status, in order to signalize the adverbial function of the phrase in relation to the sentence: *māta l'amīru wa-huwa ṣabiyy*^{un} 'the prince died while he was a boy' converts to *māta l'amīru ṣabiyyan.*

The conversion of a circumstantial clause may result in ambiguity. For the uniform marking of subordinate status, and the relative freedom of placing of an adverbial as against an adjective, mean that it may be unclear which of several entities in the main sentence is the one whose situation is described by the circumstantial phrase: *kuntu ʼalʻabu maʻa lʼamīri wa-ʼana ṣabiyyᵘⁿ* 'I used to play with the prince while I was a boy' and *kuntu ʼalʻabu maʻa lʼamīri wa-huwa ṣabiyyᵘⁿ* 'I used to play with the prince while he was a boy' both convert to *kuntu ʼalʻabu maʻa lʼamīri ṣabiyyan* 'I used to play with the prince while a boy'. This of course does not arise if there are gender and/or number contrasts between the entities.

Circumstantial clause conversion is common enough in poetry and in ancient Arabic. From the eighth century on there was a marked tendency in straightforward, non-ornamental prose to abandon it and use only the clause structures marked by *wa*. But modern writing is tending to reintroduce it into favour.

There are instances in which circumstantial clause conversion leads to a structure identical with that of substantive clause conversion after a verb of mental activity: *raʼaytu-hu wa-huwa ḍāḥikᵘⁿ* 'I (physically) observed him while he was laughing' and *raʼaytu ʼanna-hu ḍāḥikᵘⁿ* 'I (mentally) observed the fact that he was laughing' will both convert to *raʼaytu-hu ḍāḥikan*. It is, I imagine, as a result of this that a certain amount of confusion arises between the two clause structures, and the circumstantial clause structure with *wa* is not infrequently used in SA[1] to present the predicate term of a proposition functioning as object of a verb of mental activity; Muḥammad Ḥusayn Haykal writes in his *Memoirs*, *raʼaytu-hum wa-qad jāla bi-ḵāṭiri-him mā jāla bi-ḵāṭirī* ⟨I observed them in a condition where that which revolved in my mind had revolved in their mind⟩ 'I observed that the same idea had occurred to their mind as to mine'.

[1] As it was already in medieval Arabic.

13

FUNCTIONALS

The Arab grammarians group all words which are neither verbs, nor entity terms, nor nouns functioning adjectivally, under the heading of *ḥurūf* (functionals).[1] Prepositions, in so far as they can be identified as such (see p. 88), are included under this heading.

Coordination

It is essential to the nature of coordinating functionals such as 'and' and 'or', that the two speech items which they link, whether these be sentences, phrases or single words, should have exact parity of syntactic status. But two of the commonest of these functionals in Arabic, *wa* and *fa*, are ambivalent and do not always have the function of coordination; cases of non-coordinating uses of these two have already been mentioned, pp. 66, 89–90.

The basic coordinator is *wa* 'and', implying simple structural linkage. *fa* on the other hand has the additional value of implying a sequence from the preceding expression to the following one, whether temporal or logical. In temporal sequence, 'he smiled and answered' using *fa* implies that the answer followed the smile; in contrast to *wa* which allows also the possibility that the two actions may have been simultaneous. In logical sequence, the mind may progress from a cause to its effect, in which case *fa* resembles English 'so'; or from a statement back to its cause or justification, as in 'this must be true, for (*fa*) I have seen it with my own eyes'.

Subordination

A number of subordinating functionals have already been described,

[1] This also has the meaning of 'letters (of the alphabet)', and its use as a grammatical term for functionals is occasioned by the fact that some of the most characteristic members of the class consist only of single consonant plus short vowel.

including both markers of subordinate status in an entity term and indications of clause subordination.

Many subordinating functionals have an ambivalent role. *ḥattā* is not only a clause-subordinator with the values 'until', 'so that', 'in order that' (followed by a suffix set verb to denote 'so that', *a*-subset of the prefix verb for 'in order that', and either for 'until'), but has also the role of a preposition 'up to', and that of a modifier 'even' which has no effect on the sentence structure. *li* functions as preposition ('he sang for my delight') and as a clause subordinator ('he sang in order that he might delight me', p. 84).

The most interesting of the ambivalent functionals is *fa*. If this be followed by a primary set item of the prefix verb set, it is a coordinator and what follows it is a wholly independent sentence; but if followed by the *a*-subset item, and preceded by a sentence modified for negation, interrogation or command, then that modification extends to the following sentence also. The role of *fa* is thus to subordinate the second sentence to the totality of the first, so that coordination is only with the unmodified part of that. Take for example *yaṯiqūna bi-nā fa-yaʿmalūna bi-ʾamri-nā* 'they trust us, and so they do our bidding': to negative the first proposition, and use the *a*-subset in the second *lā yaṯiqūna bi-nā fa-yaʿmalū bi-ʾamri-nā*, has the sense ⟨it is not the case that {they trust us and so do our bidding}⟩ 'they do not trust us so far as to do our bidding', and implies that they do *not* do our bidding; to negative the first proposition, but retain the primary set item of the second verb *yaʿmalūna*, would establish the *fa* as having a normal coordinating role and would imply 'they do not trust us, and (yet) they do our bidding'.

Clause subordinating functionals with temporal value are in some cases nothing but substantives marked for subordinate status and employed in the structure described p. 57: *ḥīna* 'when' is the subordinately marked form of the substantive *ḥīn* 'time' (which remains a fully functioning substantive, and can be used e.g. in *hāḏā ḥīnu ʾazma*^{tin} 'this is a time of crisis'), functioning just as does *yawma* in the structure there quoted.

It is of some interest in connection with time-marking subordinators to note that a fairly sharp distinction is made between past and future time siting. An event sited in the future cannot be a fact (cf. p. 79), for it may after all not take place; consequently, 'when he comes, I will talk to him' is envisaged in Arabic as a conditional sentence, 'if-and-when (*ʾiḏā*) he comes, I will talk to him', using the characteristic conditional structure (see Chapter 14), inasmuch as the possibility remains open that he may not come.

In past time marking, a distinction has to be made between reference to a dynamic event and reference to a static situation. In reference to a static situation, such as 'when he was rich, he gave much to charity', the functional marker of the time clause is *'iḏ*. In reference to an event, the marker is *lammā*: but this nevertheless exercises on the suffix set verb (which, since an event is envisaged, is the only possible predicate in such a clause) the same kind of aspectual conversive force as *qad* does (p. 78): *lammā māta lmalik* represents 'when the king had died' or 'when the king was dead', and *not* 'when [= at the actual instant when] the king died'. Actual simultaneity of two events can only be marked by one of the substantives referred to above (e.g. *ḥīna māt*[a] 'at the time he died'), or by a preposition plus substantive clause (*'inda mā māt*[a], cf. p. 57), or by preposition plus verbal abstract (*'inda mawti-h*[i] 'simultaneously with his death').

The clarity of functional differentiation between *'iḏā*, *'iḏ* and *lammā* as outlined above is, however, impaired by the fact that there is some fluidity of usage between *'iḏā* and *lammā*. Even in the archaic period, 'when something had happened', if placed after *ḥattā* 'until', was always marked by *'iḏā* and not *lammā*; and in modern SA this marking seems to be gaining some ground in other circumstances as well, in spite of the fact that an ambiguity is thereby created between past and future time reference.

A characteristic of both medieval and SA is that an initial *lammā* clause is sometimes treated, like a prepositional phrase (p. 65), as a logical theme, in that the following main clause begins with *fa*, which is thus in this case not a coordinator and cannot be translated in English.

All three of these time functionals are, moreover, ambivalent in that they can be used to indicate causation: just as in English the properly time-marking functional 'since' can be used in lieu of 'because'.

Negation

The most generalized negative functional is *lā*, but there are others with specialized uses. Apart from *lays*[a] (on which see below), all negative functionals modifying a verb predicate immediately precede the verb, with which they are in closest juncture so as to constitute a wholly indivisible phrase; those negativing a non-verbal predicate precede the theme.

The negative reflex of a suffix set verb with static aspectual value (whether or not the positive form be explicitly marked for static aspect by *qad*, p. 78) is *lam* + the short variety of the prefix set verb. Hence the negative of *qad*[i] *ṭṭala'nā 'alā lkitāb* 'we have/had perused the book' is *lam naṭṭali' 'alā lkitāb* 'we have/had not perused the book'; and note that the latter form is in contrast with both *lā naṭṭali'u* 'we do/will/can/etc. not peruse' and *lā naṭṭali'* 'let us not peruse' (p. 84).

The suffix set verb with dynamic aspect is regularly negatived by *mā*. Unlike *lam*, this negative functional enters into other structures as well. It is in free alternation with *lays^a^* for the negation of a non-verbal predicate; with *lā* as negativing a prefix-set verb item when this depicts a situation contemporaneous with the moment of utterance; and it will sometimes be found negativing the suffix-set item of a modifying verb, in place of *lam* + prefix-set item.[1]

lays^{a} is a modifying verb showing differentiation of the agent pronoun (⟨I not⟩, ⟨she not⟩, etc.) by means of suffix morphemes only, and has no contrasting prefix set. In other respects it is structured exactly like the modifying *kwn*, including the transformation of a simple noun predicate from independent to subordinate status. But it comports only pure negative modification, not past time or notional value (owing to its lack of a prefix set which could furnish a contrast with the suffix forms), for which appropriately negatived forms of *kwn* must be used. Hence, *hāḏā ṣaḥīḥ^{un}* 'this is true', *laysa hāḏā ṣaḥīḥan* 'this is not true', but *lam yakun hāḏā ṣaḥīḥan* 'this was not true', *'an lā yakūna hāḏā ṣaḥīḥan* 'that this should not be true'. As to position, since *lays^{a}* itself has the status of a verb, the normal rule for placing of a negative is neutralized, and it can occur either before the theme (which then becomes its agent) or before the predicate: *laysa hāḏā ṣaḥīḥan* or *hāḏā laysa ṣaḥīḥan* 'this is not true'.

A simple noun predicate of a negatived proposition can be marked by the preposition *bi* in lieu of the syntactic marker of subordinate status: *mā hāḏā bi-ṣaḥīḥ^{in}*, *laysa hāḏā bi-ṣaḥīḥ^{in}*, etc.

The English structure 'no + substantive' is paralleled in Arabic by one in which an undefined substantive functions as theme (see p. 65) preceded by *lā*. The substantive in this structure has the mark of subordinate status, thus *lā taw'amayni yatašābihāni bi-ttadqīq* 'no two twins are exactly alike'; but the subordinate marker *-a* is in this case never accompanied by *-n*, hence *lā ṭabība fī lbayt* 'no doctor is in the house', not **lā ṭabīban*. This marking might well lead one to assign a verbal force to the *lā* and to envisage the parts of the sentence which follow the substantive as amplifications of it, so that the above examples are treated as 'there are no two twins who are exactly alike' and 'there is no doctor (who is) in the house'.

This analysis is nevertheless incorrect.[2] The crucial point is that the *lā* + substantive structure is never used in Arabic in isolation, and can consequently not be regarded as a valid sentence structure. If one

[1] In archaic Arabic, both *'in* and the combination *mā 'in* are freely used as alternatives to *mā* in all the latter's negative functions. These usages disappeared from the medieval language, yet some writers of today have revived the use of the negative *mā 'in*.

[2] Although I did adopt it in *Written Arabic* §9:5.

wishes to say simply 'there are no angels' one is obliged to employ the existential verb (p. 81[1]) and say *lā tūjadu malā' ika* 'angels do not exist'. Since therefore additions of some kind are necessary to constitute a sentence,[1] such additions must be regarded as genuine predicates.

In so far as an English 'no + substantive' structure functions otherwise than as theme, the negative must in Arabic be detached from the substantive and used to modify the predicate: the thematic form *lā 'aḥada yaqūlu hāḏā* 'nobody says this' is paralleled in the verb + agent structure by *lā yaqūlu hāḏā 'aḥad*^{un} ⟨not says this anybody⟩; and 'I saw nobody' is structured as *mā ra'aytu 'aḥadan* 'I did not see anybody'.[2]

On the analysis which I have suggested for the form *lā 'aḥada*, the negative functional has a syntactic status similar to that of the 'objectivizing' theme-markers such as *'inna*, *'anna* and *la'alla* (p. 64); and just as one could not use two of those functionals simultaneously, a difficulty is created over using one of them together with this type of *lā*, and the difficulty is commonly resolved by transferring the negative into the predicate part of the sentence, producing the form *yaḥtamilu 'anna 'aḥadan lā yaqūlu hāḏā* ⟨it is probable that anybody does not say this⟩ 'it is probable that nobody says this'.

The antithetical negative concept 'that which is not-X' is expressed by a noun *ḡayr* annexed to the other term of the antithesis: *ḡayr-ī* ⟨somebody/anybody who is not-me⟩, *ḡayr*^{v} *nihā'iyy*^{in} substantivally or adjectivally '(something) interminable'. This noun has certain anomalies as to definitional status. In itself it is logically undefined, though the term to which it is annexed may be defined or undefined: *ḡayr*^{v} *malik*^{in} ⟨somebody/anybody who is not a king⟩ versus *ḡayr*^{v} *lmalik*^{i} ⟨somebody/anybody who is not the king⟩. Up to the recent past, the structural requirements for defined or undefined status were met by appropriate marking of the term to which *ḡayr* was annexed, the word itself never having the article: thus *wakīl*^{v} *ḡāyr*^{v} *'ādil*^{in} 'an unjust steward', *lwakīl*^{v} *ḡayr*^{v} *l'ādil*^{i} 'the unjust steward', *lwakīlu ḡayru 'ādil*^{in} 'the steward is unjust'. But in SA a distinct tendency is emerging to mark *ḡayr* with the article when it is required to have defined status,

[1] It is true that expressions of this kind can function as sentence structures with ellipse of the predicate, as with English 'No doubt!' There are two Arabic clichés often used, both as elliptical sentence structures introduced by the coordinating *wa* 'and', and (like English 'this is no doubt true') simply as adverbials, viz. *lā budda* and *lā jarama* 'of course'/'inevitably'/'necessarily'/ etc.

[2] It may be noticed that it would be difficult in Arabic to reproduce the logical paradox exploited by Lewis Carroll in the passage concerning the Anglo-Saxon Messenger who 'saw nobody (or Nobody) on the road'.

and hence to write *lwakīl*^{v} *lġayr*^{v} *lʿādil*^{i} 'the unjust steward' which exhibits a type of contrast with the other two structures not found anywhere else in annexion structures.

Another tendency gaining ground in SA (though the first instances of it are to be found already in the medieval language) is to use *lā* in place of *ġayr* with nouns: *ġayr*^{v} *nihā'iyy*^{in} is now in competition with *lānihā'iyy* for 'interminable', and the new coinage 'decentralized' is exclusively *lāmarkaziyy* and not **ġayr*^{v} *markaziyy*^{in}.

In adjectival and circumstantial clause conversion, a negatived clause predicate is matched by *ġayr* in the conversion structure: *ʿibārat*^{v} *laysa maʿnā-hā wāḍiḥ*^{an} 'an expression of which the meaning is not clear' converts to *ʿibārat*^{v} *ġayr*^{v} *wāḍiḥin maʿnā-hā*.

In substantive clause conversion a negatived clause predicate is matched by *ʿadam* 'absence (of)' annexed to the verbal abstract: *'anna hāḏā lā yumkin* 'that this is not possible' converts to *ʿadam*^{v} *'imkāni hāḏā* 'the impossibility of this'.

Questions

All SA interrogative functionals occur at beginning of the sentence except that a preposition may precede. A statement is converted into a question by the initial functional *'a* or *hal*; these do not *necessarily* entail any other change in the sentence structure, but they *can* be accompanied by certain inversions bringing the term which is the point of the enquiry to the position of a logical theme at the beginning of the sentence, so that in this case a formal predicate can precede the formal theme, and an object term precede the verb; thus the unmodified structures *'a-'anta jāhil* 'are you ignorant?' and *'a-qulta hāḏā* 'did you say this?' are paralleled by *'a-jāhilun 'anta* which might be rendered by the Irishism 'is it ignorant that you are?' and *'a-hāḏā qulta* 'is it this that you said?'.

Interrogative entity terms 'who?', 'what?' have the same morphological shape as the specialized entity terms *man*, *mā* (p. 49). As interrogatives they can be treated structurally as themes with subsequent referential pronoun, as in *mā yadḵulu fī-hi hāḏā*? 'into what does this enter?'; or as displaced sentence elements, needing no referential pronoun, *fī-ma yadḵulu hāḏā*? (interrogative *mā* loses its vowel length after a preposition). But if anything else than a preposition precedes the queried entity, only the thematic formulation is possible: *man saqaṭa fī yaday-h*? ⟨who it fell into his hands?⟩ 'into whose hands did it fall?'.

Any interrogative sentence, structured as above, can function as an entity term in a larger sentence, principally of course as direct object of verbs such as 'ask', 'wonder', etc. The English structure 'I asked her whether she thinks so' can be structured as ⟨I asked her does she think so⟩ *sa'altu-hā 'a-tufakkiru ka-ḏālik*^{a}. But just as in English, 'whether' can be replaced by 'if', so this structure can in Arabic be replaced by one in which the queried proposition is put in conditional structure (p. 104) with the conditional functional *'iḏā*. In so far as the main verb may demand an indirect object, it will be impossible to place a clause of this kind immediately after the preposition, since a preposition cannot be followed immediately by a modifying functional; the clause must be turned into a substantive by the use of *mā* (p. 57), thus producing the common cliché *fī mā 'iḏā*, as in *šakaktu fī mā 'iḏā* 'I doubt if...'.

Emphasis

The ancient Arabic functional *la* 'indeed' survives with its original emphatic value in SA only in a few cliché phrases where it modifies a handful of predicate verbs such as *qalla* 'is rare', *šadda* 'is violent', as in *la-qalla hāḏā* 'rare indeed is this', *la-šadda ḵaṭa'u-k*^{a} 'gross indeed is your mistake'.

Otherwise, it is now only used mechanically—and quite optionally—(i) as an accompaniment of the functional *qad* (*la-qad*); (ii) to mark the beginning of a predicate when the theme has been marked by *'inna* (p. 64); and (iii) to mark the beginning of the main proposition after a hypothetical *law* clause (p. 107). In the latter two cases its value is principally structural and the modifying value of emphasis has become very weak and hardly reproducible in English; with *qad* it is wholly otiose.

14

CONDITIONAL STRUCTURES

Conditional sentences proper contain two propositions of which one conditions the validity of the other: if the conditioning proposition is validated, the conditioned one will be so also; if it is not, the conditioned proposition is also invalidated. In 'if he comes tomorrow, I will talk to him', the proposition 'I will talk to him' is a conditioned one which will not be validated unless 'he comes' turns out eventually to be valid. In the strict sense, therefore, a conditional sentence can only be sited in the future, since the open-ended possibility of a proposition being either validated or invalidated cannot truly exist in the past; when an apparently conditional sentence is sited in the past as with 'if he came yesterday . . .', its open-ended nature applies to the speaker's knowledge of the fact, not to the fact itself, which is necessarily positively determined one way or the other. But there are many types of sentence which do not conform to the strict definition of a conditional, as given above, yet show sufficient structural similarity to be grouped together as 'conditional structures'.

Both propositions in an Arabic conditional sentence are marked by a characteristic structure; the conditioning one also by a functional. The simplest of these functionals is *'in* 'if', which implies nothing more than the uncertainty of validity. *'iḏā* had originally a time significance in addition, 'if ever/if at any time/whenever', but in SA has largely encroached on the domain of *'in*. And there are other functionals used with the conditional structure, such as *mahmā* 'if . . . anything/whatever', etc.

Easily the most noticeable feature of Arabic conditional structures is a shift in the value of the verb sets: the suffix set assumes the range of meanings otherwise associated with the prefix set. The shift can occur in both propositions: a structure which, unconditioned, would have had the value 'I talked to him', assumes the conditioned value 'I will [given certain circumstances] talk to him' when brought into the context of a conditioning proposition; a structure which in isolation would have the value 'he arrived', takes on, when presented with a conditional functional as a conditioning proposition, the value of an open future possibility that he may or may not arrive, 'if he arrives'.

From this it follows that a timeless non-verbal predicate structure has no place in the strictly conditional sentence.[1] 'If he does this, he will be a fool' necessarily presents the conditioned proposition in a structure which, unconditioned, would have meant 'he was a fool'; 'if the director is free, I will talk to him' presents the conditioning proposition in a structure which, without the conditional functional, would have meant 'the director was free'. In both cases, therefore, one is obliged to use the suffix set item of the modifying verb *kwn* (p. 80).

The value shift operates mechanically and applies equally to any suffix set modifying verb whatever be the nature of the main predicate: *kuntu 'abkī* 'I used to cry' and *dumtu 'abkī* 'I went on crying' contrast with *'in kuntu 'abkī* 'if I am in the habit of crying' and *'in dumtu 'abkī* 'if I go on crying'. In order therefore to retain the original time value of a modifying verb, if this is needed, it is normal to extrapolate the modifying verb from the conditional structure altogether, leaving the mechanical value shift to operate on the main predicate verb. Observe the contrasts:

nuġādiru lbayt[a]	*nuġalliqu lbāb[a]*
'we (habitually) leave the house'	'we (habitually) lock the door'

'iḏā ġādarnā lbayta ġallaqnā lbāb
'if ever we leave the house, we lock the door'

kunnā nuġādiru lbayt[a]	*kunnā nuġalliqu lbāb[a]*
'we used to leave the house'	'we used to lock the door'

kunnā 'iḏā ġādarnā lbayta ġallaqnā lbāb
'if ever we left the house, we locked the door'

Ancient Arabic freely used an alternative to this value shift: namely the replacement of the primary prefix set by its short variety. Thus there was the contrast between *bakaytu* 'I burst into tears', *'abqī* 'I cry/am crying' and *'in bakaytu* or alternatively *'in 'abki* 'if I cry'. This alternative virtually dropped out of use in medieval Arabic, but has been reintroduced by SA writers.

These structures are obligatory in the conditioning clause; they are not so in the main proposition. But if they are not used in the main

[1] The occasional placing of an independent pronoun theme after *'in* is a structural anomaly which seems to be a survival from an archaic phase of the language, before its logical categories had become established.

proposition, the beginning of the latter is marked by *fa*. For instance, if the main proposition is a command verb, which is not susceptible of the characteristic conditional shifts, this requirement is operative: *'in waṣala kallamta-h^u* 'if he arrives, you will talk to him', but *'in waṣala fa-kallim-hu* 'if he arrives, talk to him'.

In order to site a conditional sentence in past time, it is necessary first to devise a structure which contains a prefix set verb, and yet has a past time marking, e.g. *'an 'akūna qad 'aḵṭa'tu* ⟨that I should be in the state of having made a mistake⟩: the conditional shift can then be applied to the modifying prefix set verb, producing *'in kuntu qad 'aḵṭa'tu* 'if I have made a mistake'. The same applies to the conditioned proposition.

It often happens that the logically conditioned proposition is omitted and replaced by an unconditionally valid one, as in 'if I make a mistake, mistakes do occur'. The unconditionally valid proposition is presented by *fa* plus thematic structure; the conditional shift would be unsuitable, since that would mark the proposition as only conditionally valid.

Fundamentally similar to this is the 'even if' structure, which also leaves unexpressed the logically conditioned proposition and replaces it by an unconditionally valid one: 'I shall be there, even if he doesn't come'. The original structure of such statements in Arabic has to be regarded as two separate statements: 'I shall be there, and (*wa*) if he doesn't come [that will not affect my presence]'. This has however generated structures in which 'and if' has ceased to be felt as coordinating functional + conditional functional, and come to be regarded as a functional in its own right with the value 'although'. It is therefore no longer obligatory to place such a clause after the main (unconditioned) proposition; it can be emboxed between theme and predicate of the latter, or precede the latter entirely, but the main proposition (or its predicate) which comes after the 'although' clause, begins with *fa* in older Arabic; in SA, this *fa* is tending increasingly to be replaced by an adversative coordinating functional corresponding to English 'nevertheless' or 'yet' (*wa-lākin, ḡayra 'anna*, etc.). This structure, in spite of still embodying *'in* and still exhibiting the 'conditional' shift in the clause which follows the *'in*, has lost all logical contact with conditions, since in 'although . . . yet' both propositions are unconditionally valid.

The element of uncertainty as to ultimate validation, which is present in true conditional sentences, is heightened in the 'hypothetical' sentence, which in English is marked by the contrast between the simple conditional 'if he arrives' and the hypothetical 'supposing he were to arrive', and in the main proposition by the insertion of 'would'. In hypothetical sentences sited in past time, the uncertainty hardens into a negative certainty, 'supposing he had arrived' implying that he did not in fact arrive. Arabic hypothetical sentences are not time marked, and a single structure covers both the English forms 'on the assumption of his (future) arrival, I would talk to him' and 'on the assumption of his (past) arrival, I would have talked to him'. A distinctive functional *law* marks the hypothetical conditioning clause, and in both members of the sentence a verbal sentence structure with suffix set verb is required: hence *law kāna fī lbayt* covers both 'supposing he were to be in the house' and 'supposing he had been in the house'. The beginning of the main proposition can optionally be marked by *la*.

wa-law has evolved structurally in much the same way as *wa-'in*. But it is to be observed that in both this case and that of the normal hypothetical sentence, should the main predicate be placed in front of the clause, its hypothetical evaluation will only become apparent when the clause has been reached: *kallamtu-hu law waṣal*[a] 'I would talk to him if he were to arrive', *mā kallamtu-hu wa-law waṣal*[a] 'I wouldn't talk to him even if he were to arrive'.

A minor phenomenon which has some interest as a structural survival from a primitive stage of the language, is the use of a command verb followed without a coordinator by a prefix set verb in the short form. This corresponds structurally to an unsophisticated type of utterance such as 'Give me sixpence, mister, I carry your bag'. Logically, the second proposition is a conditioned one, with omission of the conditioning clause 'if you do so'; hence no doubt the conditional use of the short variety of the prefix set (p. 105).

15

WORD ORDER

A good deal has already been said in earlier chapters about the relative placing of individual words making up a phrase or clause. This chapter is concerned with the ordering of the prime constituents of the sentence—theme, predicate and amplifications of the predicate.

Easily the most baffling problem in this connection is the factor determining the choice between a thematic structure (theme → predicate) and a verbal one (verb → agent) in main sentences; subordinate clauses to a large extent have this choice determined by grammatical considerations. It seems to be true that in literary prose the choice of a verbal sentence structure is the more favoured one, yet the thematic structure is only slightly less so, and the operative factor in the choice is still very obscure.

In the verbal sentence structure, one has to consider the relative placing of agent, object and adverbials. As has been mentioned above (p. 88), adverbials enjoy considerable freedom of placing, even to the extent of preceding the verb; in such a case, although becoming logically a theme, they are not formally so and do not require a subsequent referential pronoun (contrast the formal thematic structures ⟨the king, smote-him the pestilence on that day⟩ and ⟨that day, smote the king on-it the pestilence⟩ with the logically but not formally thematic one ⟨on that day, smote the king the pestilence⟩). An indirect object can of course be extrapolated as theme with subsequent preposition + referential pronoun (*hāḏā lkitābu ṭṭalaʿnā ʿalay-h*^{i} ⟨this book, we have perused it⟩), but the placing of an indirect object as such (i.e. the entity term with its accompanying preposition) before the verb is exceptionally unusual apart from one or two special cases (e.g. in an adjectival clause a preposition + pronoun is sometimes placed before the verb, *lkitāb*^{v} *llaḏī ʿalay-hi ṭṭalaʿnā* 'the book which we have perused').

Although the placing of agent, object and adverbial, relatively to each other after the verb, ranges over all the possible permutations, one fundamental principle applies to all cases: the entity assumed by the speaker to be more familiar to the hearer, and thus having less communication value, precedes one less familiar and hence having greater communication value. It will be seen that this principle echoes the principle of theme preceding predicate, for the theme is necessarily an entity assumed to be known to the hearer, while the predicate embodies fresh information about it, not previously available to the hearer.

The most conspicuous application of this principle is that a defined entity (assumedly identifiable by the hearer) normally precedes an undefined one, whose identity is not known to the hearer. This order is quite irrespective of the function of the two entities in the sentence: the word order ⟨shot the soldier a bandit⟩ is normal for both functional evaluations 'the soldier shot a bandit' and 'a bandit shot the soldier'.

A rhythmical factor appears also to have an effect on the word order. This is that the maximal break in the sentence should not occur much later than half way through its total length, so far as is possible. 'Length' in this connection has to be interpreted not on the phonological plane, but in terms of the number of lexical items. The maximal break occurs (i) in a thematic structure, between theme and predicate, (ii) in a verbal sentence structure, after the entity term which immediately follows the verb (irrespective of whether that be agent or object).

This principle operates so as to exclude, normally, a substantive clause from the beginning of the sentence even when it is the logical theme, as in 'the fact that my brother loves Mary is obvious'. A formulation ***'*anna* '*ak-ī yuḥibbu maryama ẓāhir* is avoided because the predicate 'is obvious' is so much shorter than the theme. It is avoided either by using a verb predicate structure *yaẓharu* '*anna* '*ak̠-ī* . . . ⟨is-obvious that my brother . . .⟩ or by the device of the forward-looking generalized pronoun theme (p. 41) '*inna-hu ẓāhirun* '*anna* '*ak̠-ī* . . . 'it is obvious that my brother . . .', or even without that by placing the simple predicate first *ẓāhirun* '*anna* . . . This last structure does occasionally occur, but is rare because it accords initial position in the sentence to an undefined term, which is felt to be anomalous; prepositional phrases on the other hand are extremely common in initial position, and consequently *ẓāhirun* in that structure is normally replaced by the partitive preposition *min* plus the generically defined category term, *min*$_a$ *ẓẓāhiri* ⟨a thing belonging to the category of the obvious⟩ which in spite of remaining logically undefined has at least the overt appearance of a defined term.

The rhythmical principle can also be clearly seen at work in a verbal sentence structure with both agent and object, of which one is amplified and the other not: the order verb → amplified term → unamplified term, which would result in the maximal break occurring immediately before the unamplified term (see above), is avoided. No matter which term is agent and which object, the amplified one follows the unamplified one. Hence, ⟨shot the soldier the rebel who was firing from the building⟩ and ⟨shot the rebel the soldier who was in command of the platoon⟩ are so structured no matter whether the rebel shot the soldier or vice versa. It does remain, however, an open question whether the determining factor here is purely the rhythmical consideration, or whether one has to take into account the 'familiarity' principle, since it could be presumed that an entity which the speaker feels to need amplification is less familiar to the hearer than one which he feels does not need any amplification.

One minor consequence of the familiarity principle is seen in identificatory predicates where one of the two terms is a demonstrative. Logically, all identificatory predicate structures should be freely reversible: 'Mary is my aunt' ~ 'my aunt is Mary', 'this is my meaning' ~ 'my meaning is this'. But the latter statement would ordinarily be structured in Arabic with 'this' functioning as theme, because the allusive nature of the demonstrative implies that it is more easily recognizable by the hearer than a term which needs overt description.[1]

In a verbal sentence structure, placing of the object before the agent is obligatory when the object term is logically annexed to the agent one and a pronoun is introduced to avoid repetition, as in the structure ⟨loved the boy his uncle⟩ described on p. 42.

Needless to say, distortions of normal prose order occur freely in verse, and in prose passages where a rhetorical effect is aimed at. But the admissible distortions are limited, and wholly unlike the extreme freedom of Latin verse in this respect. Such deviations as do occur almost always involve either (i) the placing of an adjective, which is not so firmly anchored to position immediately after the term it amplifies as it is in normal prose; or (ii) the placing of a prepositional phrase, which may occur almost anywhere in the sentence irrespective of its function. One will encounter cases in which a prepositional phrase occurs quite near the beginning of a line of verse, when its function may be to amplify the last word of the line. Probably the greatest difficulty the reader meets in verse is to evaluate the function of a prepositional phrase.

[1] Inversion of the order does indeed entail a change of meaning, since the phrase will then have an appositional structure without predicative function (*maʿnā-ya hāḏā* 'this idea of mine', see p. 43). But I believe this to be a consequence, not a cause, of the principle here stated.

16

LEXICON AND STYLE

In Arabic of all periods, the semantic spectrum of many lexical items is apt to seem to Europeans unduly diffuse. This is largely a mistake bred of the difficulty of viewing one's own language objectively, and of the fact that Arabic conceptual categories differ widely from those familiar to Europeans; the same criticism might easily be made about English by an Arab confronted with the semantics of 'high' (high seas, high road, high meat, high living, high adventure, high tension, etc.). Certainly the old-fashioned jibe that 'every word in Arabic means itself, its opposite and a kind of camel' is wholly unmerited; except in so far that the Arabs have themselves contributed to the illusion of 'contradictory meanings' by erecting this into a special branch of lexicography. It is, however, an illusion. The reality is that some words have a generalized meaning capable of taking an additional coloration from the context: *ṭarab* is 'strong emotion', and only the context will reveal whether the emotion is one of joy or sorrow; *ṭulūʿ* means 'climbing', and in ancient Arabic (though no longer in SA) could be used in contexts where 'climbing down' is envisaged and not 'climbing up'. The Arab lexicographers however have registered *ṭulūʿ* as a word with the contradictory meanings of 'ascending' and 'descending'.

The non-congruity of conceptual categories has the result that many lexical items (verbs above all) in the Arabic-English dictionary appear with what seems to the European a surprisingly disparate set of renderings. The converse is also true. Some concepts for which English has only one word are for the Arabs a series of quite independent concepts with appropriate words for each, or concepts subdivided into specialized compartments with distinctions not made in English: 'time' considered as a point or moment is for the Arab a wholly different concept from linear time, and each of these concepts has a number of specialized distinctions—under the heading of linear time one has to distinguish between *mudda*, a stretch of time considered *per se*, and *fatra*, a stretch of time considered merely as the interval between two limiting points.

Arabic has also been alleged to be unusually rich in synonyms, but it is doubtful whether it is exceptional in this respect. Most cases of alleged synonymity are at best partial, and this is a phenomenon of all languages. In seventeenth- and eighteenth-century English poetry, 'orb' and 'eye' are in free alternation provided that the human eye is in question, but it has never been possible to speak of *'the orb of a needle' or *'the king's eye and sceptre'. Arabic synonymity is usually of the same kind.

What is unusual about Arabic is the extent to which this phenomenon is countered by the device of hendiadis: the use of two words with different but overlapping semantic spectra to denote the area of overlap. To take an example at a simple level:

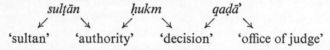

	sulṭān		*ḥukm*		*qaḍā'*
↙	↘	↙	↘	↙	↘
'sultan'		'authority'	'decision'		'office of judge'

In order to express the concept 'authority', an Arabic writer will often use *ḥukm wa-sulṭān*, in order to express 'decision' *ḥukm wa-qaḍā'*. Such expressions are in no way tautological, as they would illusorily appear to be if one attempted to render them with two English words; they represent a single concept and should be so rendered in English. Not only single words, but whole phrases, may be brought within the scope of this principle, and a true translation may have to eliminate quite large sections of Arabic.

In another direction, however, the tendency to tautology cannot be denied, but is an inheritance from very ancient times indeed, having its roots in the most ancient Semitic literature. Canaanite poetry, as exemplified in the Ugaritic poems of the second millennium B.C., and the poetic passages of the Old Testament, rely for their effect not on a prosodic structure as we know it, but on a rhythmical balance between two (occasionally three) clauses which are also marked by a careful parallelism of sense which may be one of contrast or one of similarity: phraseology such as 'all day long I weep, and in the night season I take no rest', or 'mine enemy hath overcome me and mine adversary hath gotten the dominion over me' will be instantly familiar to readers of the Old Testament. Archaic Arabic oratorical prose shows exactly the same features, usually together with the additional adornment of rhyming between the final words of each member of the parallelism. It could, in fact, be called poetry within the ancient Semitic definition, though it is not 'poetry' (*šiʿr*) for an Arab, because Arabic *šiʿr* has developed a well-defined prosodic structure based on a pattern of contrasts between the syllabic structures *cv* and *cvc*.[1] But oratorical utterances of the above-mentioned type are given the special name *saj'*, usually translated by Europeans 'rhymed prose'—not a happy rendering, because the rhyme is of less significance than the rhythmical and semantic parallelism, and without these two latter features a piece would not be *saj'*.

Although *saj'* in its pure form has now fallen out of favour, the habits of thought associated with it have left an ineffaceable mark even on contemporary writing, and even when the writer is in no way aiming at an oratorical or high-flown style. In 1968, the author of a quite straightforward academic essay writes[2]: *'ammā 'uslūbu rrasā'ili fa-fawqa 'uslūbi lmaqāmāti ṣan'atan wa-tazwīqan wa-zuḵrufan wa-tanmīqan* 'the style of the Epistles is superior to that of the Maqāmāt in artifice and embellishment and decoration and ornamentation', with the piling up of four terms which cannot be said to add much to the sense, and in addition the rhyme between *tazwīqan* and *tanmīqan*. We find a historian writing in 1960[3] that a factor leading to the weakness of the emirs was *yaqẓatu lḵilāfati ba'da ġafwatin wa-ṣaḥwatu-hā ba'da ḍu'fin wa-'iṯrā'u-hā ba'da faqr* 'the caliphate's awakening after slumber, its stirring after weakness, and its enrichment after poverty', with strongly marked structural and semantic parallelism of the three members.

Both these quotations illustrate the Arab fondness for the use of two or more terms which, while not 'synonyms' in a strict sense, are so close to synonymity as to do little towards developing the author's thought, producing a much more rhetorical style than is usual in current English. And if the thought demands the repetition of a concept, Arabic will usually try to avoid repetition of the word by using some near-synonym. On the other hand, when *structural* considerations demand the repetition of a word, it can be repeated without hesitation, as in the former quotation where English 'that of the Maqamat' is represented by 'the style of the Maqamat'.

Arabic use of pronouns borders sometimes on the irresponsible. They are freely employed without any attempt to aid the hearer in identifying which of several pronouns in a sentence refers to which of several previously mentioned entities. English use of the 'ornate epithet' to avoid ambiguity of pronoun reference ('Edward VII . . . the king . . . the monarch', etc.) is alien to traditional Arabic style, though tending slightly, under European influence, to creep into contemporary writing.

[1] A few contemporary poets have been experimenting with 'free verse', but these attempts are still something of an experiment.

[2] Māzin Mubārak in *Revue de l'Académie arabe de Damas*, vol. 43, p. 607.

[3] Ḥasan Maḥmūd, *Ḥaḍāratu miṣra l'islāmiyya, 'al'aṣru ṭṭūlūniyy*, p. 159.

Most noticeable is the still current practice of writing in elaborately structured paragraphs, rather in the manner of English nineteenth-century (and earlier) style. The modern English habit of cumulating short staccato sentences punctuated by full stops has as yet found small echo in Arabic, and it is rare in SA for a new main sentence within the paragraph not to be linked to the preceding context by a coordinating functional; even the paragraph frequently begins with 'and' (*wa* or *fa*).

Arabic has on the whole been fairly resistant to the importation of foreign words. At no period has there been such a radical transformation of the lexical stock as took place in English in the thirteenth century with the adoption of a vast flood of Norman-French words, or at the Renaissance with its Latinisms. The prevailing tendency has always been to assign new senses to existing words, or to make new coinages from the existing resources of the language; thus the modern demand for a huge new technological vocabulary, for which English has resorted to coinages mostly based on Greek, has in Arabic to a large extent been met by a policy similar to that of German, with its *Sauerstoff* 'oxygen', *Zuckerkrankheit* 'diabetes', etc. (and, earlier, the calque *Rücksicht* 'respect').

The assignment of new senses to existing words is normally by adding a new specific limitation within the generalized semantic field of the word; this has not resulted in the obsolescence of either the generalized sense or of earlier specific limitations. *ṭāʾir* has the generalized sense of 'flyer' (as substantive) or 'flying' (as adjective), and particularized senses of 'bird' and 'omen'; its modern use for 'aviator' is simply an addition of a new particularized sense within the pre-existing semantic range. The modernism *ḏarra* 'atom' (with *ḏarriyy* 'atomic') has not eliminated the older sense 'speck of dust'.

Two common methods of evolving new coinages are the use of the 'feminine' termination, and of the derivational morphemes *-iyy* and *-iyya*, for items in which they were not used at all, or at best only rarely, in the older languge: *dabbāb* 'a creeper' has generated *dabbāba* now exclusively meaning 'a tank', since 'a (feminine) creeping thing', though theoretically possible, was not in fact in usage earlier. The same is the case with the derivational terms *ramziyy* 'symbolist' and *ramziyya* 'symbolism' generated from the older *ramz* 'a sign'. Cf. also *wujūdiyy* 'existential' and *wujūdiyya* 'existentialism' mentioned earlier (p. 36). The use of participle forms for coining neologisms has previously been noted (p. 75).

In many cases, a European word coined from a compound Latinism or Grecism is represented in SA by an annexion structure. The prefix re- is rendered by *radd* 'return (of)' or *ʾiʿāda* 'repetition (of)', as in *radd*^{v} *lfiʿli* 'reaction' and *ʾiʿādat*^{v} *nnaẓari* 'reconsideration'. Most of the 'ologies' are rendered by *ʿilm* 'science of', though there are a few direct borrowings such as *jiyulūjiyā* 'geology'.

The Arab Academies of Cairo and Damascus have devoted much labour to devising new coinages from the resources of the language itself,[1] but their recommendations do not always win general acceptance. The official coinage *hātif* 'telephone' has not ousted the loanword from popular usage, any more than official German *Fernsprecher* has.

Accepted loanwords are almost exclusively substantives. Loaned verbs are very rare, but have been generated in a few cases, as with the medievally attested *faylasūf* 'philosopher' > *tafalsaf*[a] 'he philosophized' and in modern times *ʾasfalt* 'asphalt' > *saflat*[a] 'he asphalted'.

The need for a large new vocabulary dealing with technological and scientific matters is, however, the least interesting feature of the new lexical developments; more fascinating, though more elusive, is the evolution of new words for intellectual concepts. In English, words of this kind are mostly Latinisms, the semantic background of which is certainly not appreciable to the ordinary user, for whom they are 'new words' in every sense. This is far less the case in SA. It is true that the ordinary user of the now popular *taṭawwur* 'development' probably never stops to think of its evolution from the idea of 'proceeding stage (*ṭawr*) by stage'; but the relationship of *masʾūliyya* 'responsibility' to the idea of being 'questioned' (*masʾūl*) about something is too obvious to be overlooked.

There are not a few words which were rare and poetic in the older language, but have been pressed into service for modern concepts. Until modern times, an Arab might say that he knew something, or that he opined it, but the notion of 'feeling' as a conceptual category distinct from 'knowledge' and 'opinion' never entered his head. Ancient Arabic had, however, two words for 'he knew', *ʿalim*[a] and *šaʿar*[a][2]; the writers of the golden age plumped heavily for the former, and the latter became a rare and somewhat poetic word. In SA, it is the latter which has been selected for the modern intellectual concept of 'feeling' as distinct from knowledge and opinion, and it is now very common.

For the ancient Arab, the liver was the seat of the emotions, the heart of intellectual activity. But because emotion does make the

[1] See R. Hamzaoui, *L'académie arabe de Damas et le problème de la modernisation de la langue arabe*.

[2] It is true that it is arguable that there *may* have existed from the first a distinction between 'rational knowledge' implied by the former and 'instinctive knowledge' by the second; but although such a distinction would certainly have been appreciated by the golden age writers, it is to me highly doubtful whether an Arab of the seventh century would have understood it at all.

heart pound, instances can be found where *qalb* 'heart' is associated with the emotions. The SA expression *šukr qalbiyy* 'hearty thanks', though undoubtedly calqué on European usage, cannot be said to conflict radically with tradition: it is merely the elevation of a sporadic usage into a normal one.

In fact, easily the most difficult problem confronting research into modern vocabulary is that of identifying what is a 'modern' usage. I myself have time and time again discovered that a word which I had thought to have a characteristically modern sense has turned up in that sense somewhere in medieval literature. The problem arises in part from the deficiencies of Arabic lexicography. Traditional Arab lexica, as well as European works based on them (such as Lane's *Arabic-English Lexicon* and Freytag's *Lexicon Arabico-Latinum*, both classics in their way), deal practically exclusively with the ancient language. And at least one excellent dictionary, that of Wehr, deals with the modern language. But no comprehensive lexicon of mediaeval usage exists as yet; Dozy's *Supplement aux dictionnaires arabes* and Fagnan's *Additions aux dictionnaires arabes* only constitute preliminary soundings into the subject.[1]

[1] These remarks on the lexicon are purposely somewhat sketchy, because this is one aspect of SA which has received fairly comprehensive coverage, particularly in the previously cited works of V. Monteil and R. Hamzaoui.

APPENDIX: SCRIPT STYLES

The earliest specimens of Arabic script present a very rude and ungraceful appearance. Even when used for 'formal' purposes (as in inscriptions and coins) it has clearly not been moulded by artistic canons governing the proportions, etc., of the letters. But eighth-century copies of the Qur'ān already show the emergence of a scribal tradition which has imposed regular rules on the formation of the letters, producing a formalized script of considerable beauty. To this, and to various styles deriving from it, the term 'Kufic' has commonly been applied, although in fact it is now clear that these styles have no special connection with the city of Kufa in Southern Iraq.

In the ninth century a new style evolved, which came to be the standard 'copybook' style throughout the medieval period, and is termed *nasḵ* or 'copy' hand. Whereas Kufic styles are stiff and somewhat angular and spiky, the best *nasḵ* is above all characterized by graceful free-flowing curves. Normal modern type-faces are ultimately modelled on this style.

Standard copybook *nasḵ* has given rise to two further developments: the *taʿlīq* style emerging in the fifteenth century, which has become the favourite in Persia and India, though rarely used in the Arab world proper, and which carries the free sweeps of the *nasḵ* style to an even further degree; and the *ruqʿa* script which became popular in the Ottoman period and is today the normal style used for handwriting in most of the Arab world.[1] Type-faces modelled on both *taʿlīq* and *ruqʿa* are however nowadays sometimes employed for purposes of distinctiveness, rather in the same way that we might use italic type to afford a distinction from normal roman.

[1] An exhaustive account of *ruqʿa* script is found in T. F. Mitchell's *Writing Arabic* (Oxford University Press, 2nd ed., 1958).

The *nasḵ* style, however, never took root in Morocco and Algeria, where the typical Maghribi ('western') script is of Kufic inspiration, and is only in the most recent years beginning to give ground in consequence of the dissemination of books printed in the standard modern type-face.

Highly elaborate decorative styles (of both Kufic and *nasḵ* inspiration) are often used on title-pages. One common feature of these decorative scripts is a tendency to avoid blank spaces between the letters (caused by the fact that some letters of the alphabet have risers projecting above the main line of script, and others pendentives sinking below it), either by inserting a vowel mark, or by the use of dots, strokes and squiggles which are purely decorative in function and have no other significance; a feature which can be very disconcerting to a beginner.

Page 119 shows:

(i) Two lines from the contemporary poet Kamāl Naš'at in copybook *nasḵ* with the short vowel marks, etc., reading,

wa-'aḡfā[1] *ṣamtu-hā lmaḥbūbu fawqa llayli wa-l'ašjār*
wa-habbat min rawā'iḥi-hā 'uṭūru l'amni wa-l'īṯār
'and its dear silence sleeps o'er night and trees
and from its breaths waft scents of peace and love'

(ii) the same two lines in the normal modern handwriting style, *ruq'a*, without short vowel marking.

(iii) the same two lines as actually printed in the author's published poems, in a normal modern type-face without short vowel marking.

(iv) a type-face of *ta'līq* inspiration, reading

fī ṭab'atin 'ūlā sanata 'alfin wa-tis'i mi'atin wa-tis'in
wa-ḵamsīna fī lmaṭba'ati lkāṯūlīkiyya bayrūt lubnān
'first edition 1959 at the Catholic Press, Beirut, Lebanon'.

(v) title-page in ornamental script of Kufic inspiration reading

šarḥu lqaṣā'idi ssab'i ṭṭiwāli ljāhiliyyāt
'Commentary on the seven long Pre-Islamic odes'.

Those who wish to study the letter forms shown in these specimens should consult my *Written Arabic*, pp. 10–23; but it is as well to point out here the cardinal fact that the script reads from right to left.

[1] Length of the final *ā* marked by *y* and not *'alif*, see p. 27.

وَأَغْفَى صَمْتُهَا ٱلْمَحْبُوبُ فَوْقَ ٱللَّيْلِ وَٱلْأَشْجَارِ
(I)
وَهَبَّتْ مِنْ رَوَائِحِهَا عُطُورُ ٱلْأَمْنِ وَٱلْإِيثَارِ

وأغفى صمتها المحبوب فوق الليل والأشجار
(II)
وهبت من روائحها عطور الأمن والإيثار

وأغفى صمتها المحبوب فوق الليل والأشجار
(III)
وهبت من روائحها عطور الأمن والإيثار

في طبعة اولى سنة ألف وتسع مئة وتسع وخمسين
(IV)
في المطبعة الكاثوليكية - بيروت - لبنان

شرح القصائد السبع الطوال
(V)
الجاهليات

BIBLIOGRAPHY

Al-Ani, S. H.: *Arabic phonology, an acoustical and physiological investigation* (Janua Linguarum series, Mouton, The Hague, 1970). This has only come to hand when the present work was already in proof.

Bateson, M. C.: *Arabic language handbook* (Washington, Center for applied linguistics, 1967). Sets out to do something of the same sort as I have attempted in the present work; but the part of it devoted to actual linguistic structures is a great deal briefer and more summary than mine.

Beeston, A. F. L.: *Written Arabic, an approach to the basic structures* (Cambridge University Press, 1968). Based on the same type of approach as the present work, but presented in pedagogic form for students wishing actually to learn to read the language.

Cantineau, J.: *Etudes de linguistique arabe* (Paris, Klincksieck, 1960). Of crucial importance for the professional linguist, specially in the field of phonetics.

Chejne, A. G.: *The Arabic language, its role in history* (University of Minnesota Press, Minneapolis, 1969). Chapters 6 ('The revival of literary Arabic in modern times') and 8 ('Problems and proposals for the reform of Arabic') are of relevance to the student of contemporary Arabic.

Gairdner, W. H. T.: *The phonetics of Arabic* (Oxford University Press, 1925). In spite of its age, this is still valuable; but it has to be remembered that, in so far as not concerned with the Egyptian vernacular, it has its main emphasis on the 'high classical' style used in the recitation of the Qur'ān.

Hamzaoui, R.: *L'académie arabe de Damas et le problème de la modernisation de la langue arabe* (Leiden, Brill, 1965). Useful account of the academy's contributions to the creation of lexical neologisms.

Harrell, R. S. and Blanc, H.: *Contributions to Arabic linguistics* (Harvard Center for Middle Eastern Studies, 1960). Harrell's contribution, 'A linguistic analysis of Egyptian radio Arabic', is the best work available on SA forms, but presupposes a pretty thorough previous knowledge of Arabic.

Magee, W.: 'Pronunciation of prelingual mutes in classical Arabic', in *Word*, vol. 6, pp. 74–7.

Monteil, V.: *L'arabe moderne* (Paris, Klincksieck, 1960). Extremely valuable, but (like Harrell's work cited above) it presupposes a previous familiarity with Arabic, being principally devoted to describing how the modern idiom differs from the older language.

Obrecht, D. H.: *Effects of the second formant on the perception of velarized consonants in Arabic* (The Hague, Mouton, 1968).

Pellat, C.: *Introduction à l'arabe moderne* (Paris, Maisonneuve, 1956). Granted that its methodological approach is that of traditional grammar, this is perhaps about the best practical learner's manual.

Wehr, H.: *A Dictionary of Modern Written Arabic*, Ed. J. M. Cowan (Wiesbaden, Harrassowitz, 1961). The only Arabic–English dictionary of any use to students of the modern language.

Ziadeh, F. J. and Winder, E. B.: *An introduction to modern Arabic* (Princeton University Press, 1957). A useful practical manual based on the 'direct' approach by analysis of illustrative texts.

INDEX